Epochal Discordance

SUNY SERIES IN
CONTEMPORARY CONTINENTAL PHILOSOPHY

Dennis J. Schmidt, editor

EPOCHAL DISCORDANCE

Hölderlin's Philosophy of Tragedy

VÉRONIQUE M. FÓTI

STATE UNIVERSITY OF NEW YORK PRESS

Published by
STATE UNIVERSITY OF NEW YORK PRESS
ALBANY

Printed in the United States of America

For information, address
State University of New York Press
194 Washington Avenue, Suite 305, Albany, NY 12210-2384

Production, Laurie Searl
Marketing, Anne M. Valentine

Library of Congress Cataloging-in-Publication Data

Fóti, Véronique Marion.
Epochal discordance : Hölderlin's philosophy of tragedy / Véronique M. Fóti.
p. cm. — (SUNY series in contemporary continental philosophy)
Includes bibliographical references (p.) and indexes.
ISBN-13: 978-0-7914-6859-3 (hardcover : alk. paper)
ISBN-10: 0-7914-6859-3 (hardcover : alk. paper)
ISBN-13: 978-0-7914-6860-9 (pbk. : alk. paper)
1. Hölderlin, Friedrich, 1770-1843—Philosophy. 2. Tragedy—Philosophy. I. Title. II. Series.

PT2359.H2F68 2006
809.2'512—dc22

2005030810

10 9 8 7 6 5 4 3 2 1

For my sons and daughters:

Sunil Sharma, Leila Sharma,
Ravi K. Sharma, Amina Sharma

Contents

We must ask from the gods

things suited to hearts that shall die,

knowing the path we are in, the nature of our doom.

—Pindar, *Pythian* III, trans. C. M. Bowra

Prefatory Note

All translations from the German and French are my own, unless otherwise indicated. Translations from the Greek are based on the Greek texts cited and, where indicated, on other translations consulted, which have for the most part been modified.

In citing Greek names, I have generally rendered the letter *kappa* by *k*, rather than by the Latinized *c* (thus, for instance, Kreon); but in the case of names that are almost invaribly cited with Latinized spelling, such as those of Sophocles and Empedocles, I have left the *c* in place.

Prologue

> Excess dominates, which is why there must be tragedy, limits by default. . . . [The moderns] no longer had access to the transports which carried the Greeks beyond themselves: we are barbarians to the point of seeing Dionysian excess as mere barbarism.[1]

It is astonishing that this book—completed, as it happens, almost exactly two centuries after the publication (in April 1804) of Hölderlin's Sophocles translations—remains one of the first two efforts to study Hölderlin's thought on tragedy as a whole from the three fragmentary versions of his own tragedy, *The Death of Empedocles*, and the body of essays on the poetics and philosophy of tragedy connected with it, to the late translations (or, more properly, linguistic transpositions) of two of Sophocles' three Theban plays, together with the hermetic "Remarks" he appended to them. There exist, to be sure, a number of excellent specific studies (particularly in the German and French scholarship), published mostly as chapters in edited or authored books; yet only one other scholar, Françoise Dastur, so far has undertaken to trace Hölderlin's itinerary of thought *in tragoediam* (his *Denkweg*, as Heidegger might say), even though the question of the tragic forms the vital and sensitive nerve of his thought.[1]

The further task this book sets itself is to read Hölderlin's analyses of tragedy as they demand to be read: as philosophy, rather than as the "theoretical" reflections (or worse: the oracular pronouncements) of a significant, but difficult, poet. Hölderlin, classically educated, a painstaking reader of Kant, student and critic of Fichte, and friend of Hegel and Schelling, was deeply involved in philosophy; and his own philosophy of tragedy is integral to (and may, in fact, have largely motivated) the "tragic turning" in German philosophy, which stretched from the close of the eighteenth century to Heidegger's analyses near the midpoint of the twentieth century. Hölderlin's fragmentary

Empedocles tragedy and his Sophocles translations are, to be sure, works of literature; but they rest on a philosophical foundation, which he took care to elaborate and clarify.

Hölderlin's thought on tragedy is not closed in on itself, but stands in vital interconnection with that of other thinkers, ranging from Empedocles (who, of course, did not write about Attic tragedy [although he is said to have composed tragedies of his own], but who, in his philosophical poem *Katharmoi*, or *Purifications*, presents his understanding of the tragic fate suffered by the spirit or *daimōn*) to Hegel, Nietzsche, and Heidegger. The question of the tragic penetrates the thought of these modern and contemporary thinkers to its core, as it does that of Hölderlin.

This is one reason why no single study can hope, after all, fully to encompass Hölderlin's thought on tragedy, not only in its textual and intellectual scope, but in all its complex ramifications in the wider panorama of philosophy and literature. A further reason is that such an encompassing project would also require a detailed scholarly analysis of Hölderlin's Sophocles translations, on which, as yet, little work has been done. During the writing of this book, I (who will here lay aside the academic author's mask of quasi-anonymity to speak in the first person) have had the experience of a recurrent, quasi-visual image. The image was one of scintillating light flashing forth in the pure colors of the spectrum at some otherwise inconspicous point—the sort of sudden flashes of color one might see in a drop of dew or on an icicle touched by the winter sun (I must leave the contemplation of faceted diamonds to wealthier authors). At almost every point the issues treated seemed similarly to scintillate; and one could have followed out multiple trajectories of questioning. I trust, however, that the reader will, on the whole, find such sparkle more stimulating than the blank whiteness (or, on the analogy of a pigmentary mixture of colors, the dull grey) that would have resulted from seeking to integrate and to resolve absolutely everything. Perhaps the reader will herself or himself be stimulated to follow out some of the questions that are allowed to flash forth.

In this Prologue, I will indicate just two or three of the points at which the light breaks. Firstly, whereas Hegel situates tragedy, or tragic conflict and its resolution, within ethicality (*Sittlichkeit*, as a surpassed self-actualization of spirit), Hölderlin decisively withdraws it from the ethical domain. In this, he is followed by Nietzsche and Heidegger, as well as by Reiner Schürmann (who, however, dismisses his thought on the basis of a cursory and questionable reading, taking his own guidance from Nietzsche and Heidegger). The twisting free of tragedy from the grip of Hegelian ethicality does not mean that the concerns normally classed as ethical are cast to the winds (a reproach too often made to Heidegger), but rather that they are resituated against a vaster horizon—the horizon, perhaps, of what lies "beyond good and evil," of the dispropriative trait in the propriative event (*Ereignis*), or of the tragic structure in the instauration and despoilment of hegemonic principles.

If these characterizations roughly indicate the wider horizon as understood by Nietzsche, Heidegger, and Schürmann, how does Hölderlin understand it? One cannot offer a rough characterization here, for, even though his ethical and political vision (succinctly articulated in his character Empedocles' final testament in the tragedy's First Version) remains constant, the horizon against which it articulates itself does not. Just how to interpret its changing configurations? These range from Hölderlin's initial exaltation of nature's primordial elements (indebted, not to the Latin principle of *natura*, but to Empedocles' elemental "roots"), which so far has not been commented on in the interpretive literature, to—firstly, but not finally—the idea of the destinal sacrifice of an exceptional individual as demanded by an epochal transition or "turning of the times." The notion of an essential sacrifice, which also informs Hegel's early thought on tragedy and which can be traced as a rather cryptic locution in several Heideggerian texts, consitutes another point of scintillation, which will merely be noted here without further comment.

Hölderlin, however, goes on to repudiate the speculative and perhaps religiously inspired thought-structure of the sacrifice of "time's first born" (without ceasing to link tragedy to an epochal transition). The horizon for understanding tragedy becomes, in the end (at the final tragic turning or *Umkehr*) that of the sheer finitude of mortal experience, of a temporality without issue, and of an affirmation of this earth. A question that flashes forth is how this affirmation can arise from one's being thrown back, in suffering, upon what Hölderlin refers to as the empty form of time (a specter, perhaps, of Kant's understanding of time as an *a priori* form of intuition), which leaves "beginning" and "end" in irremediable, atelic, and counterspeculative discordance. What is the full import of this radical temporal incoherence and fragmentation, which subverts the schema of speculative thought? It will not admit, for instance, of an originary yet still withheld beginning, a beginning that is yet to be realized, as Heidegger thinks it in his understanding of the historicality of Western thought. More generally, how could human life configure itself ethically, or also creatively, in Hölderlinian temporal discordance? Must and can such discordance be modified without denying the conflictual structure of the real that is fundamentally at issue in tragedy?

A second and important point of scintillation can perhaps be envisaged from the perspective of the idea of reconciliation. Whereas, for Hegel, reconciliation remains the guiding aim of tragedy and defines its cathartic work, the late Hölderlin sees ultimate reconciliation—the reconciliation of man with divinity—not as the ideal of a differential interrelation, but as a hybristic union, destructive of the singular, and motivated by "eccentric enthusiasm," which is fundamentally a passion for death. The cathartic work of tragedy therefore becomes for him a work of dispersive separation.

One context in which this separative work gains special importance is that of the historical relationship between Greece and Hesperia (the name by which Hölderlin, who links Greece to the East, refers to the West). Hölderlin's analysis here turns on distinguishing, in both cultures, between natal endowment and formative drive (*Bildungstrieb*). Greece and Hesperia stand in a chiasmatic complementarity in that the Greek formative drive strives for the sobriety, lucid articulation, and plastic power that constitute Hesperia's natal endowment, whereas the Hesperian formative drive cultivates what is natural to the Greek spirit: a fiery passion, intensity, and grandeur that verge on devastating excess. Only through an assiduous cultivation of what is alien to it, in keeping with its own formative drive, can either culture come to learn the free and sovereign use of what is genuinely its own; for a consummate actualization of one's ownmost gifts is, as Hölderlin stresses, far from spontaneous or natural. At the same time, however, the formative drive, having achieved a high perfection of its ideal, can then come to define a culture, as Greece tended to be defined by what Nietzsche called its Apollonian traits, masking its natal tendency to Dionysian excess.

This implies, firstly, that any attempted *mimēsis* of ancient Greece will always be deflected by coming up against the self-alienating force of the Greek formative drive and so will be incapable of reaching "Greece" itself, which shows itself to be a phantom. More importantly, however, such a mimetic relationship, blindly pursued, will, in Hölderlin's view, prove dangerous. It is tragedy that reveals this danger in that it *presents* (but does not itself enact) the breaking free of the searing Greek fire from the restraints and limits imposed on it by the Greek formative drive, as a failure of the restraining and purifying impulse from which, in his view, Greece ultimately perished (along with its tragic art). Hölderlin here presents a very different view of the death of tragedy (in the context of the perishing of Greek classical culture) than does Nietzsche, for whom tragedy perished, not of unpurified Dionysian excess, but of the exaltation of theoretical reason. If Hesperia should now seek blindly to imitate Greece, it will find itself drawn fatefully into maximizing the impassioned excess that constitutes the Greek natal endowment. This happens due to the orientation of Hesperia's own formative drive, which strives for what is lacking in the natal gift proper to Hesperia: passion, grandeur, and a sense of destiny.

If sobriety and lucid articulation are pursued to excess, they become pedantry and cultural sclerosis (it is against the latter, as an excess of the Greek formative drive, that Antigone, on Hölderlin's interpretation, rebels); but the Greek fire, maximized by the Hesperian quest for a mimetic union with Greece, becomes an encompassing and destructive conflagration.

The question that flashes forth here concerns Hölderlin's premonition, if such it was, of the dangers looming on the still-distant Hesperian horizon, and the self-critical vigilance that he therefore demanded of intellectual life. His warning certainly has not been heeded and probably was largely not understood. Today, however, one still needs to ask oneself how to configure the ineluctable relationship of contemporary philosophical thought to that of ancient Greece. The idealization of Greece, which invited a mimetic paradigm, has, to be sure, seen its day; but then again Heidegger, who initiated a new responsive engagement with Greek thought (including tragedy), has tended, in casting "the Greeks"[2] as "a people of poets and thinkers," to veil the tendency of the culture toward impassioned excess, which Hölderlin, as well as Nietzsche, were acutely sensitive to. It remains an open question how to engage, in particular, with Greek tragic thought, without either relegating it, with Hegel, to an essentially surpassed form of spiritual life, or else effacing Hesperia's differential separation from it, which Hölderlin regarded as salutary.

Now, however, lest one's eyes blur or tire, it is time to look away from the play of scintillations and to lay the sparklers aside. It is time then to turn to the texts themselves, and to enter upon the patient but challenging labor of reading which this book proposes to undertake.

ONE

The Tragic Turning and Tragic Paradigm in Philosophy

> Let us also reread that, at Aulis, [Agamemnon's] function as commander defines and universalizes him, that he inserts it into a world that is meaningful, but that also, at Aulis, the undeniable—yet denied—allegiance to his offspring likewise singularizes him. The other prescription expels him in advance from the world of arms and ships: a world that, in sacrificing his daughter, he plainly exalts as normative. The denied prescription makes non-meaning penetrate into the universal meaning. To think this double prescription for itself is to make tragic knowing one's own.

Toward the close of the eighteenth century, tragedy, which had been of scant interest to philosophers since Plato and Aristotle, began to move to the forefront of German thought. Not only was this tragic turning of philosophy sustained well into the nineteenth century, it also surfaced anew in the first half of the twentieth century in the work of Martin Heidegger. Whereas Plato and Aristotle were concerned with the question of the educational and political impact of tragedy, or with its poetics, the German thinkers focused not so much on tragedy as a dramatic form (although Hölderlin took pains to study it as such, and Hegel does explore it in his *Lectures on Aesthetics*), but on the very essence and philosophical thought-structure of the tragic, and ultimately on the role of the tragic paradigm in philosophy. Although such a focus is not wholly alien to the therapeutic concern that runs throughout much of the Western philosophical tradition—a concern for the assuaging of human suffering through a discipline of thought (here the interest of German Idealism in Spinoza is relevant, although Spinoza's thought did not directly motivate

Hölderlin's work on tragedy[1])—the tragic turning of German philosophy is unique and striking enough to provoke a quest for an explanation. Miguel de Beistegui and Simon Sparks offer one that is perceptive and thought-provoking: tragedy, in their interpretation, offered the prospect of bridging the abyss between natural necessity and human freedom, or between pure theoretical and practical reason, that yawned in the wake of Kant's critical philosophy.[2] Enticing though this analysis is—particularly in the way it revisits the Kantian sublime as "the site of the presentation of the unrepresentable"—its preoccupation with the issue of freedom responds primarily to Schelling's theory of tragedy (which nevertheless is given no place in de Beistegui and Sparks's edited volume),[3] rather than to the tragic thought of Hegel, Hölderlin, Nietzsche, or Heidegger. Most conspicuously, the analysis does not address the prominence of the question of history or historicity in the tragic turning of philosophy from Hölderlin and Hegel to Heidegger, and beyond. It also does not seek to clarify in any way the striking prominence of Sophoclean tragedy in German philosophical discussion; for, notwithstanding Hegel's interest in Aeschylus's *Oresteia* and in Shakespearean tragedy, German Idealism remained almost obsessively preoccupied with two of Sophocles' three Theban plays: *Oedipus Tyrannos* and *Antigone*; and Heidegger sustains this preoccupation. Euripides, cast by Nietzsche as a destroyer of Attic tragedy, is otherwise accorded hardly a mention; and a range of characters familiar to the Greek tragic stage, such as Ajax, Herakles, Medea, Helen, or Hekabe (Hecuba) receive little or no attention.[4] One wonders then just why only these very few plays have been selected out of the vaster legacy of Greek tragedy as speaking to and even definining the philosophical question(s) at issue, and, if so, what the implications may be of this restriction concerning the relationship between ancient Greece and modernity.

These critical reflections are not meant as a preamble to a fuller explanation of the tragic turning of philosophy. The question of what is philosophically at stake in this turning is one that may still have to be left open, not least because the issues are not the same for Hölderlin, Hegel, Schelling, Nietzsche, and Heidegger. This book does not seek to offer a comprehensive explanation, but rather to undertake an in-depth study of the tragic thought of Hölderlin. The task that this first chapter sets itself is to delineate key aspects of the tragic turning and to interrogate the formulation of a tragic paradigm in the interest of situating Hölderlin's thought in its philosophical context.

If Plato, in *Republic* X, offered the tragic poets a chance to be readmitted to and reintegrated into the *polis*, provided that they could defend their art from a philosophical vantage point trained on ethical life,[5] it is Hölderlin who could truly have responded to the Platonic challenge (and who, in fact, was deeply concerned with integrating the poet's art, not of course into the *polis*, but into Hesperian and, specifically, German modernity). Hölderlin's poetic stature should not blind one to his philosophical erudition, acumen, and creativity. However, given the history of the reception of Hölderlin's work,[6] it has taken a long time for him to begin to be given his due as a thinker. This is particularly true of English language philosophical discussion, which has tended to relegate Hölderlin's thought to the wider parameters of Heidegger scholarship, or else to its intersections with literary theory (here Dennis J. Schmidt's reading constitutes a welcome exception).[7] This book seeks then to give Hölderlin's thought on tragedy the philosophically searching reading that it demands, given that it is not only integral to the tragic turning within German Idealism (and may, in fact, have initiated it), but that it also, in important ways, challenges the tragic matrix of Idealist thought.

HEGEL'S TRAGIC PARADIGM

The origins of the tragic turning of philosophy remain partly concealed, due to the personal and ephemeral character of Hegel's and Hölderlin's intellectual interactions during their joint residence in Frankfurt (1797–1798) and during Hölderlin's subsequent first Homburg period (1798–1800). In July 1795 and in April 1796, Hölderlin also had significant interactions with Schelling. It was Schelling who, in the Tenth Letter of his *Letters on Dogmatism and Criticism* of 1795–1796, first gave tragedy philosophical prominence; but, as Schmidt notes, tragedy never really permeated his thought or formed its very nucleus, as it did for both Hegel and Hölderlin.[8] Hölderlin's response to Schelling's *Letters*, in correspondence with Immanuel Niethammer (in whose *Philosophical Journal* the work was published), does not pick up on the question of tragedy; for Hölderlin was, at the time, preoccupied with a critical reflection on Fichte's thought and with the writing of his epistolary novel *Hyperion*. He writes:

> Schelling, whom I saw before my departure [for Frankfurt], is glad to contribute to your journal, and to be introduced through you to the learned world. We did not always converse with one another in accord, but we did agree that new ideas could most lucidly be presented in the format of letters [Hölderlin had, in the preceding paragraph, noted his own plan to write a work to be titled "New Letters Concerning the Aesthetic Education of Man."] He has followed, as you will know, a better path with his convictions, before having reached his goal by the worse path [he took earlier]. Do tell me your judgment about his newest things.[9]

From 1797 to 1799, Hölderlin worked intensively on his own tragedy, *The Death of Empedocles*, and on the body of theoretical and philosophical essays interspersed between the second and third of its three fragmentary versions.[10] It is clear from this body of writings that, as concerns the philosophical formulation of the question of tragedy, Hölderlin took the lead over Hegel during this period. Hegel's first discussion of tragedy appears only in his

1802–1803 essay on natural law;[11] and a fuller treatment had to await the *Phenomenology of Spirit* of 1807, and finally the *Lectures on Aesthetics*, given in Berlin between 1820 and 1829.[12]

In the essay on Natural Law, Hegel argues for the equal right of the singular and the whole within "the reality of ethical life [*Sittlichkeit*] as absolute in-difference." As Szondi points out, his argument is directed against the rigid opposition between law and individuality in Kant's Second Critique and in Fichte's *Foundations of Natural Law*.[13] For Hegel, the absolute, integral character of ethical life can be realized only through conflict and sacrifice, which brings about a dynamic reconciliation:

> [R]econciliation consists namely in the recognition of the necessity, and in the right, which ethicality [*Sittlichkeit*] gives to its inorganic nature, and to the subterranean powers, in that it leaves to them and sacrifices a part of itself . . .[14]

This sacrifice is what brings about the tragic purification (Aristotelian *katharsis* reinterpreted) of *Sittlichkeit*.

Hegel moves on to consider corporeity in the context of tragedy. In the conflict that divides "the dual nature of the divine in its form [*Gestalt*] and objectivity," the former frees itself from the death of the latter by sacrificing its own life, which is indissociable from the latter. By this sacrifice, death is vanquished. Seen from the perspective of "the other nature" (objectivity), however, the negativity of its own power is now sublated through a living union with divinity, so that:

> The latter shines into it; and through this ideal [*ideelle*] being-one in spirit, makes it into its reconciled living body [*Leib*] which, as body, remains at the same time within difference and transitoriness and, through spirit, contemplates [*anschaut*] the divine as something alien to itself.[15]

One hears an echo of this concern for tragic corporeity in Hölderlin's "Remarks on Antigone," where he remarks that the purification or *katharsis* of the "infinite enthusiasm" that draws the human being into seeking an immediate union with the divine is accomplished differently in Greek and Hesperian tragic presentation (*Darstellung*). In the former, but not in the latter, the "tragic word" seizes the actual body, driving it to kill. Hölderlinian *katharsis*, unlike its Hegelian counterpart, ultimately does not accomplish union or reconciliation, but separation.[16]

More immediately, Hegel shares with Hölderlin, at this early period, a focus on sacrifice as the proper work of tragedy. However, for Hölderlin, the sacrificial death of his tragic protagonist, Empedocles, is not offered up for the living unity of ethical life, but rather is called for by a turning of the times (*Zeitenwende*) or epochal transition. Empedocles' historical moment is characterized, in Hölderlin's view, by the extreme antagonism of Art and Nature, or of the organic and aorgic principles (the latter is echoed in Hegel's reference to the "inorganic"). Empedocles' apocryphal self-immolation in the volcanic crater of Mt. Aetna, however, is not an unproblematic act of reconciliation. Rather, it atones for a reconciliation that was precipitous and "excessive" in that the protagonist had sought to accomplish it in his own personal life. As a tragedian, moreover, Hölderlin brings the different perspectives of various characters to bear on this sacrificial act, thus calling it into question. Whereas Hölderlin sustains his linkage of tragedy to a time out of joint, together with his understanding of the separative force of tragic purification, beyond his work on *The Death of Empedocles* and into his translations and transpositions of Sophoclean tragedies during his second Homburg period (1804–1806), he seems to have come to repudiate the idea that the sacrificial death of an extraordinary individual could be demanded by and set on course an epochal transition. This repudiation probably accounts for his abandonment of *The Death of Empedocles*.

Hegel, in his essay on Natural Law, turns not to Sophocles, but to Aeschylus, specifically to *The Eumenides* in the *Oresteia* trilogy. The confrontation between the Eumenides or Furies as "powers of law, which resides in difference" and the "indifferent light" of Apollo before the ethical (*sittlichen*) organization of Athens is unable to bring about their reconciliation. It takes Athena, the city's patron divinity, to restore Orestes to Apollo, who had himself "entangled him in difference" (by commanding him to avenge the murder of his father with matricide). By separating out the powers that converged in Orestes' sacrilege, she now accomplishes their reconciliation; and she allows the Eumenides to share in divine honors and in the contemplation of divinity, and thus to be calmed. Tragedy's essence, Hegel concludes (before moving on to a consideration of comedy[17]) lies in the fact that:

> Ethical [*die sittliche*] nature separates from itself its inorganic [aspect] as a destiny, so as not to be entangled with it, and sets it over agains itself and, by recognizing it in strife, is reconciled with the divine being [*Wesen*] as the unity of the two.[18]

In contrast to Hegel's focus on Aeschylus's *Eumenides* in the essay on Natural Law, in the *Phenomenology of Spirit*,[19] his analysis of the spiritual truth of ethicality (*Sittlichkeit*) and of the spiritual work of art is trained on Sophocles' *Oedipus Tyrannos* and *Antigone*, especially on the latter work since, as Hegel remarks, ethical consciousness is more complete, and its guilt more pure, "when it *knows in advance* the law and the power, which it opposes, taking it for violation and wrong, for ethically accidental, [and] when, like Antigone, it commits the crime knowingly."[20] Oedipus, by contrast, acts in ignorance, so that here ethical consciousness is shrouded by "a power that shuns the light."

Sophoclean tragedy, for Hegel, explores the diremption, contrariety, and conflict within ethicality, which is lived through as a destiny culminating in the equal perdition of both contestants and, ultimately, in the historical surpassing of ethicality as a particular form of spirit. For this reason, tragedy is not, for Hegel, intrinsically timeless but is itself historically situated, or, as de Beistegui comments, it seeks to make sense only of Greek ethicality, so that "it cannot be a question of reading these pages from the *Phenomenology* as the absolute's last word on the ethico-political. . . ."[21] Similarly, Klaus Düsing notes that, for Hegel, Greek ethicality, as expressed in tragedy, is the ethicality of the heroic age, and that, within modern ethicality (characterized by a distinction between free subjectivity and the objectivity of action), the Greek model of tragedy no longer has a place.[22] This relegation of tragedy to the past contrasts sharply with Hölderlin's efforts in *The Death of Empedocles* to write a tragedy on a Greek theme for his own age, and in the Sophocles translations to transpose Greek tragedy into a poetic form capable of speaking to the historical situation of Hesperian modernity.

The diremption within the historical actuality of spirit as ethical substance (as which it realized itself in Greek civilization) divides it into general and singular self-consciousness, manifest as the people or the state on the one hand, and as the family on the other, which constitute, respectively, the spheres of human and of divine law, and within which, again respectively, man and woman function as their "natural self and active individuality."[23] Since ethicality as such remains general or universal, the family, as the immediate and natural ethical community, seeks fundamentally to elevate the singular individual who belongs to it to universality. However, Hegel argues, "the action which encompasses the entire existence of the blood relative . . . [and which] has him as its object and content as a universal [*allgemeines*] being, lifted beyond sensuous, that is, singular reality, no longer concerns the *living*, but the *dead*."[24] The universality which the singular reaches naturally and as such is "pure being, death;" but since such natural universality is devoid of consciousness and conscious agency it is the duty of family members to transmute this mere natural event into conscious agency, and thereby "to lift up the powerless, pure *singular* singularity to *general individuality*."[25] The family carries out this duty, which is the sole one mandated toward the individual by divine law, through the burial rites whereby it restores (literally, "marries") its deceased member to "the womb of earth, the elementary, imperishable individuality," thereby allowing the individual to share in a community (*Gemeinwesen*).[26]

One can perhaps hear an echo here of the communion of Hölderlin's Empedocles with the primordial elements (among which fire, not earth, is preeminent and also associated with death); but Hegel's emphasis on death and burial rites runs counter to the resistance to the passion for death (*Todeslust*) that marks Hölderlin's late thought on tragedy. Indeed, a key change in Hölderlin's thought between *The Death of Empedocles* and the late Sophocles translations is that nature and its primordial elements are no longer experienced rapturously in a longing for union, but rather as "the course of nature, ever hostile to man," which is oriented toward "the wild world of the dead." The "more genuine Zeus" of Hesperia forces this course "*more resolutely toward the earth*," which is, for Hölderlin, not the element that receives the dead, but rather the abode of the living.[27]

The woman who, within the family, most fully embodies divine law or the obscure powers is not, for Hegel, the wife, the mother, or the daughter—all of whose familial relationships involve natural affection, indebtedness, or passion—but the sister, specifically the sister of a brother. Her relationship to him is one of free equality; and through the recognition she offers to and also receives from him, she forms a bond with his alterity and singularity. For this reason, Hegel argues, he is for her strictly irreplaceable; and her familial duty toward him is her highest duty.

Human law, or the powers that prevail in the clarity of day are, on the other hand, most fully individualized in those who exercize rulership (and who, in the Greek context of ethicality, were men). The ruler constitutes "*actual* spirit, reflecting itself into itself, the simple *self* of ethical substance in its entirety."[28] The ruler can grant the ruled a certain latitude and autonomy (which allows the family to thrive); but he must ultimately hold them together in unity and guard them against a reversion from ethicality to natural life.

In ethicality as a whole, these constituent powers rest in harmonious balance, which is maintained by justice. Justice sustains the complementarity of what is intrinsically divided in that it comprises both the ruler's impartial enforcement of human law and the claim to redress advanced by an individual whose spirit has been violated. A person is violated by being objectified or reduced to a thing; and this reduction is most starkly the work of death, so that the redress called for coincides here with the divine law mandating appropriate burial.

This balance within ethicality, however, has so far been delineated without taking account of individual self-consciousness, which must realize itself in action. As self-consciousness, ethical consciousness directly and decisively embraces what it understands to be its naturally apportioned duty, opposing it to the claims of the contrary power. These may appear to it as willful, hybristic, and sacrilegious (as Kreon's edict appears to Antigone), or as stubborn disobedience (as Antigone's stance appears to Kreon).

Ethicality or *Sittlichkeit* differs from a modern understanding of moral life by acknowledging no intrinsic difference between knowledge and action. However, once individuality, in seeking to realize itself in action, embraces one law and pits it against the other, it brings about the disruption of ethical balance, for which reason there can then be no innocent action. Moreover, since individual action does not suspend the contrariety of ethical substance, but rather violates one of the contraries, it is transgressive or criminal.

Ethical consciousness must recognize its guilt; but since the *pathos*, in accordance with which it affirmed and enacted one of the opposed laws, is in fact its very character (for within ethicality the individual does not achieve true singularity), it cannot recognize its guilt without giving up its very character and effective actuality, which means that it perishes. What is called for, however, is not a one-sided subjugation; for Hegel concludes: "Only in the equal subjugation of both sides is absolute right accomplished, and ethical substance, or all-powerful just *destiny*, has made its appearance as the negative power, which devours both sides."[29]

In following Hegel's thought so far, it has already become apparent that the tragic paradigm, as it delineates itself in the initial tragic turning of philosophy, is far from unitary. Whereas Hegel articulates it in the context of ethicality, law, and the history of spirit, Hölderlin thinks it in the context of the human relation to divinity, of time and historicality, and, in particular, of the historical interrelation between Greece and Hesperia. The tragic *nefas* is, for Hegel, a one-sided pathos that disrupts the integral wholeness of ethicality, whereas for Hölderlin it is a precipitous rush to a union with divinity that violates the differential character and finitude of mortal existence and that must be purified, not by destruction, but by the painful moment of "unfaithfulness" in which divinity and man fail one another. The Hegelian *pathos* of the ethical individual drowns the claims of the opposing law in forgetfulness (Hegel is fond of the metaphor of the waters of Lethe); but the pain of faithlessness, or of the mutual abandonment of divinity and man, is, Hölderlin emphasizes, burnt indelibly into memory.

Whereas Sophoclean tragedy offered to Hegel an opening unto spirit's historical self-realization as ethicality, he returns to tragedy as such, in its full reality as a poetic and performative work, in the section of the *Phenomenology* devoted to the spiritual work of art.

In the concentrated sparseness, intensity, and directness of tragic drama, rather than in the narrative distance and dilation of the epic, spirit is able to represent the intrinsic duality of ethical substance "in keeping with the nature of the concept [*des Begriffs*]."[30] The tragic characters or heroes are at once "elementary *general* beings and self-conscious *individualities*," revealing themselves through a discourse which is not only free of the dissipation, contingent character, and idiosyncracies of ordinary speech, but which also expresses their conscious and lucid grasp of the inner truth of their actions, and of the *pathos* which motivates them.[31] They do so over against "the *general* ground" of choral commentary. In contrast to Nietzsche, who will criticize an interpretation of the tragic chorus as bringing the spectator on stage and who will recall for philosophy the orgins of tragic drama in sacred dance,[32] Hegel straightforwardly understands the tragic chorus as the voice of the people and of the elders, as mirroring back the spectator's representation (*Vorstellung*), and also as the source of the tragic emotions of terror and pity.[33]

In tragic representation, the contrariety within ethical substance also articulates itself as the contrast between knowledge and ignorance, as these inform action. As Hegel explains:

> The agent takes from his character his purpose and knows it as ethical essentiality; but through the determinacy of character, he knows only one of the powers of substance, and the other is for him concealed. Present reality is therefore other [as it is] in itself and [as it is] for consciousness.[34]

These moments are represented as the divine figures of Apollo (whose prophecies are deceptive or misleadingly formulated precisely because the knowledge that he stands for is also a not-knowing, or a nonacknowledgment of the whole), and of the Erinys (the Fury), a chthonic power who stands here for what lies hidden, and for the right of the violated. Zeus, as the divine form of substance itself, represents "the necessity of the *interrelation*" of the two and thus the balance and repose of the whole. Therefore, Hegel comments, tragedy initiates the "depopulation" of the divine or mythic realm which, in his characterization, appears to be a movement toward monotheism:

> The self-consciousness which is represented in [tragedy] thus knows only one highest power, and this Zeus alone as the power of the state or of the hearth and, within the contrariety of knowledge, [him alone] as the father of the knowledge of the *particular* that is taking form—and as the Zeus of the oath and the Erinys, of the *general* [as] of the inwardness that dwells in what is hidden.[35]

Hegel's Zeus, as the figure of the wholeness of ethical substance, contrasts with Hölderlin's figure of "the more genuine Zeus," who does not preside over a surpassed spiritual-historical configuration, but who, within both modernity and Hesperia, resists death-bound passion and brings about a return to and appreciation of "this earth" and of the measures of finitude. If this Hesperian Zeus remains nevertheless a Greek divine figure, one must consider here Hölderlin's comment to Friedrich Wilmans (the publisher of his Sophocles translations) concerning the ideal of Greek simplicity:

> I believe I have written throughout against eccentric enthusiasm, and thus to have attained Greek simplicity; I also hope in the future to remain with this principle . . . against eccentric enthusiasm.[36]

In the Greek formative passion or *Bildungstrieb*—but not (as will be explained in subsequent chapters) in the natal endowment of the Greek spirit—Hölderlin discerned a power of resistance to a death-impassioned "enthusiasm" that he, perhaps prophetically, sensed on the Hesperian horizon.

In the *Lectures on Aesthetics*, Hegel abandons an exclusive focus on the essentiality and thought-structure of the tragic (as well as the comic), offering instead a comprehensive and searching analysis of drama (for him the highest form of poetry, and thus of art as such), and of tragedy in particular. He examines not only the distinctive characteristics of drama (as compared to epic and lyric poetry), along with the qualifications of the dramatist (he must show openness and encompassing breadth of spirit), but also the poetics of drama, its theatrical production, effects on the audience, classical and modern types, and finally the concrete forms that tragedy and comedy may achieve within the framework of these distinctions.

As concerns tragedy, Hegel identifies its originary and guiding principle as the truth of divinity—not, however, in its intrinsic repose, but as realized in the world, through the *pathos* of individual agency.[37] In this form, spiritual substance is ethicality (*das Sittliche*).

Since the *pathos* that guides individual action becomes manifest as a power that disrupts the balanced totality of ethical substance, it provokes the opposed *pathos* and power. The essence of the tragic, however, lies not only in the mutual violation and guilt that both powers necessarily incur, but in the fact that, in their "collision," they are both intrinsically and equally justified. Hegel comments:

> Only thus do things truly get serious with those gods who . . . abide in their peaceable calm and unity, now when they really have come to life as the determinate *pathos* of a human individuality, [and] lead, all justification notwithstanding, to guilt and wrong in virtue of their determinate specificity [*Besonderheit*], and the opposition thereof to [its] other.[38]

This conflict, however, cannot maintain itself as the truth of substance, but must sublate (*aufheben*) itself, which requires the perdition of the tragic characters or antagonists. The truth of substance does not, Hegel stresses, lie in "one-sided specificity," but in *reconciliation* (*Versöhnung*); and it is through reconciliation that tragedy offers a vision [*Anblick*] of eternal justice.[39] Hegel's emphasis here is on reconciliation as the proper work of tragedy, which, as already indicated, contrasts with Hölderlin's focus on its work of *separation*, or of turning divinity and man away from an impassioned and precipitate union with one another. In this context, Hegel comments on the Aristotelian *katharsis* of the emotions of fear or terror and pity to the effect that what purifies them is a shift in their content, so that fear becomes trained on the ethical power which is at once a determination of free human reason and eternal and inviolable, while pity is no longer mere condolence, but recognizes and affirms the justice of the tragic character's suffering.[40]

In modern, and specifically Romantic drama, Hegel points out, a concern with subjectivity and personal passion displaces the ancient thematic of ethical right and necessity. Nevertheless, and particularly in tragedy, the course of action must reveal a certain intrinsic necessity, attributable perhaps to providence or destiny.[41] In comparing Greek and modern drama, Hegel explicitly limits his discussion of the former to Aeschylus, Sophocles, and Aristophanes (Euripides, he thinks, verges on sentimentality). Unlike Hölderlin, he summarily dismisses the East (which certainly had its own great dramatists, such as Kalidasa) as having failed to realize the principles of individual freedom and self-determination, or of "the free right of subjectivity."[42] He once again relegates classical tragedy, in its concrete development, to the heroic age and revisits the chorus and individual *pathos* as the twin aspects of the representation of ethical agency, manifesting "the non-divided consciousness of the divine, and the strife of acting which, however, appears as divine power and action, [and] which carries out ethical purposes."[43] The chorus, Hegel now stresses, is not merely the reflective spectator, but ethicality in its immediate, still unitary reality. Even though historically it evolved from the sacred origins of Greek tragedy (being specifically linked to the Dionysian cult), and even though this origin is in tension with the mythic content of Attic tragedy, the chorus remains essential to its modality of representation. In contrast, any attempt to reintroduce the chorus into modern tragedy is incongruous, since here the action does not issue from an originary, undivided consciousness.

At its purest, the conflict that drives the action arises between the state, as ethical life in its spiritual universality, and the "natural ethicality" of the family, as happens in *Antigone* (which Hegel characterizes rapturously as "the most excellent, satisfying work of art").[44] It may, however, also take other forms, such as that of an opposition between what a person consciously intends to do and what in fact he or she does without conscious awareness or intention (the obvious example given are Sophocles' two Oedipus tragedies). The true development of the action, Hegel concludes, is the sublation of contrariety, or the reconciliation of the powers in conflict, so that the tragic fate and suffering of the protagonists reveals its rationality, and the spectator finds herself reconciled to it. Quite apart from its historical closure, then, classical tragedy, as Hegel understands it, is also subjected to a *philosophical* closure which allows for no ultimately incomprehensible and unreconciled negativity, nor for what Hölderlin will refer to as the bare recounting, in suffering, of the empty measures of time.

In modern tragic drama, by contrast, action is not motivated by ethicality, but by purely subjective purposes, while the characters, who are psychologically far more developed, reflect inexhaustible human diversity. They often lack inner clarity and steadfastness and are given, instead, to vaccillation and discord. A tragedy driven by these subjective factors is, Hegel finds, more saddening and distressing than intellectually satisfying; and poetically the development of a character in terms of "the formal necessity of [his or her] individuality" is preferable (his example is the old King Lear's progression from doting folly to madness). Modern tragic drama accomplishes no reconciliation capable of revealing "eternal justice." When justice is done, it is of a more abstract and coldly legalistic nature (thus Goneril and Regan in *King Lear* are punished cruelly but appropriately). The outcome of the action, however, may not be the result of any sort of justice, but merely of unfortunate circumstances and twists of fate (in which case there is no reason why it could not just as well be fortunate).[45]

In sum, then, modern drama has necessarily exceeded the classical thought-structure of the tragic. This does not, of course, keep it from reaching sometimes unparalleled literary heights, as it does, in Hegel's judgment, in Goethe's *Faust* (which he characterizes as "the absolute philosophical tragedy") or in Shakespearean tragedy (he singles out *Hamlet*, in particular, to comment on). It also does not keep it from continuing its important work of confronting systematic philosophy with the challenge of the negative, even though it can no longer do so within the parameters of ethicality.

NIETZSCHE'S "OPTICS" OF TRAGEDY

When the young Nietzsche entered into the tragic turning of philosophy with *The Birth of Tragedy* (published in 1872 and preceded by several closely related, unpublished essays),[46] he broke with Hegel's then-dominant interpretation and redefined the tragic paradigm for philosophy. This rethinking is indebted not only to the important influence of Jacob Burckhardt, who had called attention to the sinister forces at work in the Greek *polis*,[47] but also and above all to Nietzsche's intensive reading of Hölderlin. Like Hölderlin, he had attempted (in 1870–71) to write a tragedy centered on the figure of Empedocles (it did not advance beyond a cluster of plans); and it is also intriguing that "Philosophy in the Tragic Age of the Greeks" breaks off at the threshold of addressing the thought of Empedocles.[48] This discussion will focus only on *The Birth of Tragedy* since the larger question of Nietzsche's ongoing rethinking of the tragic, and particularly of the figure of Dionysos, would demand a separate study.

Whereas Hölderlin had, in his Sophocles translations, affirmed the continuing life of Greek tragedy and sought to make it speak to modernity, Nietzsche, like Hegel, recognizes the death of tragedy. Although, in *The Birth of Tragedy*, he envisaged its possible rebirth out of the spirit of (Wagnerian) music, he castigates himself in the distanced retrospect of his "Attempt at Self-Criticism" for "tying hopes" to what left nothing to be hoped for and for his advocacy of a music that he came to consider not only as "the most un-Greek of all possible art forms," but also as dangerous due to its being "an intoxicating and, at the same time, *befogging* narcotic."[49] Yet it remains true that the fundamental concern of *The Birth of Tragedy* itself is the phoenix-like rebirth of tragedy and the need of modernity for this rebirth.[50]

For Nietzsche, the death of tragedy did not just follow from the exhaustion (or dialectical surpassing) of ethicality; tragedy died violently and, indeed, in a tragic manner.[51] It perished by "suicide," at the hands of the last of the great tragedians, Euripides, who not only prepared the way for its successor, new Attic comedy, by popularizing its formal and exalted diction, but who, on a deeper level, sought in vain to make intellectual sense of its recalcitrant mythic material, together with the work of his predecessors. Euripides, as Nietzsche understands him, was one of those rarest of artists he speaks of in the "Attempt at Self-Criticism" (and who, he notes, might have formed the proper audience for his own book), in that he was both a highly gifted creator and an incisive analytical thinker.[52] As such an artist, Nietzsche remarks, even Euripides was perhaps still only a mask for divinity; but the god speaking through him was "not Dionysos, nor yet Apollo, but a wholly newborn demon called *Socrates*.[53] In the terser language of the "Attempt at Self-Criticism," tragedy perished of "the Socratism of morality, of dialectic, of the contentment and serenity of theoretical man."[54] This indicates that it did not really die once and for all in antiquity, but that its death throes prolonged themselves certainly right into the Hegelian analysis. Tragedy's work—its very life, as Nietzsche understands it—is stifled in being cast as a work of reconciliation that culminates in the sublation of contrariety within ethical life. Its proper work is one, not of reconciliation, but of presentation.

What tragedy presents is ultimately Dionysian truth, which is inherently conflictual, given that the Dionysian and Apollonian primordial art energies (which recall Hölderlin's aorgic and organic energies or principles) require one another; they can come fully into their own only in an intimacy of strife.[55] In the "Attempt at Self-Criticism," Nietzsche therefore emphasizes that morality (*die Moral*) or "the *moral* interpretation and significance of existence [*Dasein*]," which suppresses contrariety in its quest for justification and reconciliation, is hostile to life, given that life is "essentially amoral." Along with morality or (Hegelian) ethicality, he castigates the scientific attitude (*die Wissenschaftlichkeit*) as "a fear of and flight from pessimism," and thus as a ruse against truth.[56]

Nietzsche characterizes the "pessimism," which he stresses in the "Attempt at Self-Criticism" (and which figures in the very title of the 1886 edition which includes this self-critical preface), as a "pessimism of strength" which shrinks from nothing and which springs, not from depressive weariness, but from exuberant vitality:

> Is there perhaps a pessimism of *strength*? An intellectual pre-disposition for the hard, the terrible, evil, problematic [aspects] of existence, out of its [own] wellbeing, overflowing health, its *plenitude* . . . a testing courage of the sharpest view which *demands* the horrible as the worthy enemy?[57]

Such a courageous vision, however, would be seared and blinded were it to gaze nakedly into the abyss; for "awful night" is no less destructive to sight than is the solar brilliance.[58] If perhaps the dancing "dark, colored spots" or after-images that appear in response to excessive brightness are a healing antidote, the same, Nietzsche reflects, can be said of the luminous projections (*Lichtbilderscheinungen*) that, for one who has gazed into the abyss, configure the tragic hero. They constitute an Apollonian mask whose beauty allows tragic truth to be envisaged.[59]

Rather than viewing art under the distorting "optics" of theoretical knowledge, Nietzsche proposes to view theoretical reason itself under the optics of art and art, ultimately, under the optics of life, given that "all life rests upon semblance, art, deception, optics, a necessity of the perspectival, and of error."[60] Therefore, it is art that is "the properly metaphysical activity of man;" and (against Hegel, for whom art is an essentially surpassed self-realization of spirit), "the existence of the world is justified (*gerechtfertigt*) only as an aesthetic phenomenon." Even morality or ethicality must ultimately be viewed as an appearance (*Erscheinung*).[61] One might perhaps say (although Nietzsche does not put it that way) that morality, at its best, consummates an art of living that lets its character as an artful creation and appearance shimmer through its perfected forms.

As Nietzsche explains, with reference to Raphael's painting *The Transfiguration of Christ*, appearance or luminous semblance (*der Schein*) is, at its most fundamental and preartistic level, a sheer reflection (*Widerschein*) of the traumatized vision expressed by the mythic saying of Silenus (to the effect that it would be best for humans not to be born, and second-best to die soon), or of "the eternal contradiction [echoing the Heraclitean *polemos*] that is the father of all things." Humans are caught up in this reflection in that they are constrained to experience it as physical reality, and as their own (illusional) substance."[62]

What allows a transfigured, visionary "new world of appearance" (*visionsgleiche neue Scheinwelt*) to emerge from and to redeem the primary reflection of discordant Dionysian truth is the Apollonian art impulse, generative of "a world of beauty" and dependent upon measure, limit, and the self-knowledge enjoined by the Delphic oracle. The supposedly naïve classical artist (personified above all by Homer) creates out of an utter self-dedication to and absorption in this visionary world. With this "mirroring of beauty," consummated by Homer, Nietzsche comments, "the Hellenic 'will' fought against the talent for suffering and for the wisdom of suffering [which is] correlative to artistic talent."[63]

Only after a protracted strife between the Dionysian and Apollonian energies (which, with each major new form of Hellenic art, enhanced one another through their mutual challenge) could their "mysterious marriage" ensue and give birth to Attic tragedy (Nietzsche personifies this "child" as at once Antigone and Cassandra).[64] This marital union, however, did not reconcile or neutralize the antagonism of the two principles. In Günter Figal's characterization, it constituted a particularly successful yet momentary working through of their strife, which allowed them distinctly to come into their own and reveal themselves. In an achievement of a full reconciliation, art itself would die; for, as Figal puts it, this would "annihilate the appearance which nevertheless sustains [art]."[65] The promised union is then forever postponed; and, as David Farrell Krell puts it, upon such proposing and postponing "hangs the fate of the Dionysian philosophy as a whole, as of every philosophy of ephemeral unification and inevitable dissolution."[66]

The Greek tragedies that, for Nietzsche, are paradigmatic do not include *Antigone*. They are Sophocles' two Oedipus tragedies and Aeschylus's *Prometheus*. In *Oedipus Tyrannos*, Nietzsche calls attention to the sovereign serenity that results from following the intricate dialectical process by which the protagonist attains self-knowledge—a serenity that mitigates the horror of the myth. In *Oedipus at Colonus*, this same serenity becomes supernaturally exalted; it transfigures the aged Oedipus's sheer passive exposure to suffering into "highest activity," whereas his earlier active stance as a solver of riddles and a decisive ruler only ensnared him in passivity. In this resolution of the seemingly inextricable "knot" of the Oedipus myth, Nietzsche sees "the divine counterpart of dialectics." However, the resolution remains part and parcel of the projected image, the healing phantom of light that conceals the myth's deeper import: namely that Dionysian wisdom is destructive of nature as well as of the natural self.[67] This deeper truth recalls the "passion for death" that is the destructive pull of Hölderlin's aorgic principle.

The Prometheus myth, by contrast, exalts the glory of active transgression, of the hybristic pride of the artist who challenges and rivals the gods. Aeschylus, with his characteristic concern for justice, or for the sovereignty of apportioning Moira, seeks metaphysically to reconcile the "two worlds of suffering," that of the transgressor and that of the violated gods. However, his poetic interpretation of the myth is once again a luminous and ethereal image mirrored "in a black lake of suffering." The Dionysian insight expressed by the Prometheus myth concerns the titanic drive to carry finite individuals or singular beings "higher and higher," beyond any defining identity and (Apollonian) measure. This transgressive drive entails the necessity of suffering. Even though Aeschylus is, in his concern for justice, an Apollonian artist, his *Prometheus*, Nietzsche finds, is ultimately a Dionysian mask.[68]

Nietzsche, it must be acknowledged, considers the Prometheus myth to be "the property of the entire Aryan community of peoples," casting the Oedipus myth as "Semitic," due to its supposed focus on sin and on a fall. Matters are certainly not improved by his further assimilation of "Aryan transgression" to the figure of man, and of "Semitic sin" to that of woman. However, the fundamental Dionysian import of both myths, uniting them in their mutual opposition, underlies his further statement that between them "there exists a degree of familial relation as between brother and sister." The tangled interrelation of the two paradigmatic tragic myths with a fundamental duality of "peoples" and with sexual difference constitutes a more recalcitrant knot than the one Nietzsche finds resolved in *Oedipus at Colonus*.[69]

It is interesting, finally, that the Prometheus myth, as the myth of the creator and artist, is centered on the theft and gift of fire—the element which Hölderlin's Empedocles exalts and with which he seeks to unite himself in death, whereas, in his "Remarks" on Sophocles, it has become the emblem of a searing desolation. For Nietzsche, fire remains the symbol of "the best and highest humans can share in," of the radiance of human achievement. He speculates that early humans would have considered man's disposition over fire, previously received reverently as a heavenly gift, to be sacrilegious. Thus, fire, for Nietzsche, marks both an active and creative transgression and the punishing pain that such a transgression or sacrilege necessarily entails. In this conjunction he finds "the ethical basis for pessimistic tragedy."[70] Unlike Hölderlin's conflagration, Nietzschean fire, though searing, burns brightly and does not lay waste.

TWO TWENTIETH-CENTURY PERSPECTIVES: HEIDEGGER, SCHÜRMANN

Heidegger is the one major twentieth-century thinker to have engaged with Hölderlin's thought and work as a whole, in particular his thought on tragedy, not in the interest of scholarly interpretation, but of orienting his own philosophical itinerary. Given this special intellectual relationship, his two explicit and searching discussions of Sophoclean tragedy, in *Introduction to Metaphysics* of 1935 and in the 1942 lecture course on Hölderlin's hymn *Der Ister*,[71] are examined in the concluding chapter of this book. Of these significantly different analyses, only the second, focused exclusively on the first *stasimon of Antigone*, is informed by a dialogue with Hölderlin, whereas the first, which is concerned with the intimate interrelation between being, unconcealment, and *Schein*, as both radiant appearance and semblance, is indebted to both Schelling and Nietzsche. In this initial analysis, Heidegger turns to the first *stasimon* of *Antigone*, with its focus on *technē* and the limits set to it, only after having already, if briefly, discussed Oedipus, in *Oedipus Tyrannos*, as a figure of the extremity of the Greek passion for the unconcealment of being, or of "the strife [*des Kampfes*] for being itself." This strife is enacted, for Heidegger, within the domain of knowledge or of intellectual discipline (*Wissen* and *Wissenschaft*); and he cites, in this context, the Hölderlinian saying that King Oedipus may have had "an eye too many."[72]

It will be instructive to see (in chapter 7, below) the transformative force of Heidegger's meditation on Hölderlin's reading of Sophocles as concerns his own understanding of Attic tragedy (and of the question of the tragic in relation to both Greek and German thought); but one must bear in mind that these two explicit analyses do not suffice as the textual basis for a full study of the question of the tragic or of tragedy in Heidegger's thought. Such a study can, of course, not possibly be undertaken here. Suffice it to remark that the textual basis it would require is not limited to works that, however briefly or even obliquely, refer to tragedy. Schmidt offers a detailed account of these, which is valuable in that it places them in historical as well as biographical context. He comments interestingly on Heidegger's quotation, in his rectoral address of 1933,[73] of a single line from Aeschylus's Prometheus, to the effect that *technē* is weaker than necessity although, somewhat strangely, he does not relate this citation on Heidegger's part to Nietzsche's privileging of *Prometheus* as the tragedy of the transgressor as a creator (that is, a practitioner of *technē*), and thus as supposedly the paradigmatic Aryan tragedy. Certainly this consideration would be relevant in the context of the rectoral address as well as in relation to the prominence of the issue of *technē* in Heidegger's discussion of *Antigone*.

In commenting on *Oedipus Tyrannos* in *Introduction to Metaphysics*, Heidegger remarks that:

> The space, as it were, that opens up in the inter-involvement of being, unconcealment, and radiance/semblance [*Schein*], I understand as *errancy* [*die Irre*]. Semblance, deception, delusion, errancy stand in a determinate relation of essentiality and historicality.[74]

This passage immediately recalls Heidegger's poignant analysis in his 1933 essay "On the Essence of Truth" ("Vom Wesen der Wahrheit"), of the ineluctability or error and errancy which, along with the 1942/43 lecture course on Parmenides, would be profoundly relevant for a fuller analysis of the tragic in Heidegger's thought.[75] The latter text includes a discussion of *Oedipus at Colonus* and of awe (αἰδώς) in Pindar (who is an essential poet for both Hölderlin and Heidegger);[76] furthermore, both of Heidegger's explicit discussions of tragedy are closely entwined with readings of Parmenides. A further text that would arguably be especially relevant (although it does not mention tragedy) is the 1946 essay (written on the occasion of the twentieth anniversary of Rilke's death) "What are Poets for?" ("Wozu Dichter?"), in which Hölderlin is characterized as "the pre-cursor of poets in a destitute time."[77] Concerning Hölderlin's position for Heidegger, Otto Pöggeler's comment concerning the *Beiträge zur Philosophie* (*Contributions to Philosophy*)—which would also be indispensable to a textual dossier on the tragic in Heidegger's thought—is particularly relevant:

> Heidegger's real major work, the still unpublished [at the time, in 1988] *Beiträge zur Philosophie* of 1936–1938, are determined by a conversation with Hölderlin. They want to lead out of the externalizations and omissions of the time by building a "precinct" [literally, an "ante-courtyard," *Vorhof*] in

which Hölderlin's word can be heard. 'The historical determination of philosophy,' say the *Beiträge*, 'culminates in the recognition of the necessity of making Hölderlin's word heard.'[78]

Given the focus of this study on Hölderlin's philosophy of tragedy, however, rather than on Heidegger's reading of Hölderlin, or on the mediating role of that reading for the philosopher's own understanding of the tragic, it will be necessary to resist the temptation to enter upon a study of any of the indicated texts. The one Heideggerian text that will nevertheless be considered here, if only in part, as a kind of supplement to the 1935 and 1942 texts to be examined, is "The Saying of Anaximander" of 1946. The conception of the essence of the tragic that Heidegger articulates here, with reference to Anaximander's διδόναι . . . δίκην . . . τῆς ἀδικίας, carries forward his discussions of the tragic in Sophocles.[79]

Beings, Heidegger writes in "The Saying of Anaximander," come into their own as cast into errancy ([*sind*] *in die Irre ereignet*); and "errdom" (a coinage to correspond here to Heidegger's usage of the German *Irrtum*) is instituted by being itself as the essential domain of history. Every epochal coming-into-its-own of a world-configuration is an *epochē* of being, and as such necessarily an epoch of errancy.[80] While the notion of errancy recalls, of course, its thematization in "The Essence of Truth" and in *Introduction to Metaphysics*, Heidegger here also characterizes the ec-static character of *Dasein* (or human being) as its responsive relation to being's epochal granting and self-withdrawal.

The early Greek (and, for the Occident, still, in a certain sense, future) experience of being which Heidegger finds articulated in the Anaximander fragment is the experience of presencing or manifestation as a passage out of emerging (γένεσις) into absconding (φθορὰ), so that what tarries (*weilt*) in presencing does so only as drawn into a double absencing. However, the presencing of beings is pervaded by *adikia* or the failure of *dikē*, which Heidegger thinks, not as a failure of justice in the juridical sense, but as an insurrection on the part of the singular against this temporalization and its own utter transience. Beings crave abiding presence or "the constancy of continued existence,"[81] and they do so insofar as they are released into errancy. Nonetheless, beings also find themselves constrained, by the very time-character of their presencing (by the truth that they are not, as Heidegger puts it, inserted like slices of presence between segments of absence, but are temporal through and through, and thus incapable of sheer presence) to grant *dikē* (διδόναι . . . δίκην), and thus to overcome *adikia*. This is the experience of being which Heidegger now calls "tragic," commenting that, to trace the very essence (*Wesen*) of the tragic, one must think the being of beings (τὸ ἐόν, in the Archaic Greek Heidegger privileges here), such that the beings that come to presence (τὰ ἐόντα) do so ultimately in letting the fugue-like fitting (*den fugend-fügenden Fug*) of *dikē* prevail.[82]

Heidegger (who subtly reinterprets the grammatical structure of Anaximander's fragment, as compared to readings ranging from Nietzsche's to John Burnet's) stresses that, together with the granting of *dikē* (which they do not grant to each other) beings are also constrained to grant to one another *tisis*, which he understands as considerate esteem, and for which he chooses, as a translating term, the archaic German noun *Ruch*: they cede to one another the privilege of coming to presence.

But then to what do they grant *dikē*? In answering this question, Heidegger interprets Anaximander's notion of τὸ χρεών as "the oldest name in which thinking brings being to language."[83] What comes to language in this notion is that being "hands over" presencing to what comes to presence, while also keeping it "in hand" (it is not possible here to enter upon the etymological reflections by which Heidegger supports this interpretation, or upon his translating German and Latin terms). If presencing then happens in accordance with (κατὰ) τὸ χρεών, it accords with the relational draw (*Beziehung*) by which being both releases and claims what comes to presence. Heidegger finds this thought of τὸ χρεών, which (although in a still inchoate way) thinks being and beings in their differing, akin to the thought of *Moira*, the One, and *logos* in the thought of Parmenides and of Heraclitus, and he also hears its resonance in the Platonic notion of *idea* and in Aristotle's *energeia*.

If the experience of being articulated here is tragic in an essential sense, it might seem that Heidegger's understanding of the tragic has come to repudiate the ethical domain of action or of human destiny. This appearance, however, is superficial; for an oblivion of the differing within manifestation—the differing that the tragic thought of being seeks to bring to language—is, for Heidegger, at the root of the rampant totalization (which he discusses as "the single will to conquer" and as the errant confusion or *Wirre*) that afflicts contemporary world history. It will be instructive to see, in considering his discussion of tragedy in the 1942 lecture course, how his understanding of *dikē* and of the tragic has altered and deepened in "The Saying of Anaximander."

It may seem somewhat surprising to turn, in this context, to Reiner Schürmann as a late-twentieth-century theorist of the tragic and tragedy given that, in *Des hégémonies brisées*, he dismisses Hölderlin rather summarily as a thinker who fails to recognize tragic singularization or the conflictual character of presencing; and he does so on the basis of little more than a brief and casually interpreted quotation.[84] As a consummate interpreter of Heidegger,[85] however, Schürmann may find himself in the wake of Hölderlin even when he repudiates him. More importantly, tragedy retains, for Schürmann, its contemporary philosophical relevance, so that his work constitutes, in this respect, an answer to a question Simon Sparks raises with reference to Walter Benjamin's view that tragedy has reached its epochal closure. Can one really, Sparks asks, exclude tragedy from philosophy without "passing all too quickly over the trace of the tragic which would lie at its origin?"[86]

For Schürmann, tragedy offers both a model and a module (in the sense of an intensification in a concentrated format) of the conflict (*le différend*) between the contrary impulsions of natality and mortality that, respectively, maximize and fracture the *archai* or governing principles which, as "hegemonic phantasms," are the ultimate referents of a given epochal configuration of meaning. In *Des hégémonies brisées*, Schürmann searchingly examines three such epochal phantasms: the Greek principle of the One (with reference to Parmenides and Plotinus), the Latin principle of Nature (in Cicero, Augustine, and certain medieval thinkers), and the modern principle of the subjectivity of consciousness (with reference to Luther and Kant), together with the discordant temporalization that, for Heidegger, is the tragic origin that dispropriates hegemonic phantasms. Schürmann's constellation of texts examined for each epoch is intended to juxtapose those that inaugurate the epochal configuration with those that subvert it.

Hegemonic maximization of an epochal principle is accomplished at the cost of cutting all ties with the singular phenomena that the principle is informed by, for, to function as an *archē*, it must render itself inaccessible to any possible experience. In contrast to this de-phenomenalization (under the aegis of which the singular becomes the particular, a mere instance or exemplification), mortality singularizes: "It renders us essentially alone, estranged, silent. And in haste, for it is mortality—being-toward-death—which constitutes temporality. . . . Mortality renders us familiar with our *singularization-to-come*."[87]

Mortality erodes any governing hegemonic principle or law in the manner of what Schürmann characterizes as a destabilizing and withdrawing undertow. The integrative violence of the establishment of a phantasmatic principle is thus counteracted by the dissolving violence of singularization, so that, as Schürmann puts it, "the tragic knowledge [*savoir*] of the conflict has as its content the legislative-transgressive fracture.[88]

The tragic hero, Schürmann stresses, comes face-to-face with, and is thus forced to see, binding laws in conflict (and leaving no alternative), as Aeschylus's Agamemnon finds himself under a double and irreconcilable obligation to the Argive navy that he commands and to Iphigeneia, his daughter. He confronts an ineluctable nomic conflict between a certain principle of effective governance and concern for the men under his command, and a singular familial bond. No sooner, however, does Agamemnon confront this double bind in agony than he "resolves" it by an act of forcible self-blinding (an act which, whether metaphoric, as in *Agamemnon*, or physically enacted, as in *Oedipus Tyrannos*, recurs in Greek tragedy). Agamemnon blinds himself to one of the laws in conflict, or to the claim it has upon him (predictably to the one that concerns a woman and the familial sphere), and he brazenly sacrifices his daughter. His denial shows an inherent escalation in that it is itself denied: from one moment to the next he pronounces it right and good to sacrifice the girl; he sees and treats her as though she were a sacrificial goat (the animal symbol of tragedy); and agony cedes to audacity.

Tragedy, Schürmann notes, traces out a line of sight—or perhaps rather (as this book argues in its analyses of Sophoclean tragedies) of its loss and its restoration at the point where a deliberate but partial self-blinding has become an encompassing and inextricable blindness, the point of *atē*, which is at once delusion and disaster. Only at this point is blindness transmuted into tragic insight, or into a visionary recognition of discordant temporalization.

If the model and module of tragedy remains philosophically pertinent today, the reason is that, as Schürmann writes:

> No age, before our own, has known planetary violence. None, therefore, is in a better position to unlearn phantasmatic maximization, to learn the tragic condition, and to hold on to it. A privilege which itself is a *deinon*. The task, then, of grasping how violence is born of a trauma that thought inflicts on itself will not exactly be disinterested.[89]

Although no brief and summary discussion can hope to do justice to the complexity of Schürmann's posthumous book (and even though he repudiates Hölderlin), these remarks will perhaps have succeeded in indicating the parameters against which Hölderlin's philosophy of tragedy needs to be situated today. It is time, therefore, to engage now with Hölderlin's thought.

TWO

Communing with the Pure Elements: The First Two Versions of *The Death of Empedocles*

> Cycling again and again over the alphabetic ground . . . the film [Hollis Frampton's *Zorns Lemma*] gradually replaces each "letter" with a fragment of landscape that . . . takes on the character of a pure emblem. . . . Indeed, the first four substitute images—reeds, smoke, flames, waves—capture a thought of the real as primordial separation: earth, air, fire, water. And behind that separation, as its very condition of being, is light.

Hölderlin wrote to Ludwig Neuffer from Homburg on 4 June 1799 that he had completed his tragedy, *The Death of Empedocles*, except for the last act, and that he expected to publish it in the literary periodical (*Iduna*, named for the ancient Germanic goddess of dawn) that he was seeking to found.[1] To his half-brother Karl Gok, he wrote on the same day of the "slow love and effort" he had been devoting to the work; and he laboriously copied for him most of Empedocles' monologue from act 2, scene 4 of the Second Version.[2] In September 1799, however, he wrote to Susette Gontard that his plan for the literary journal had failed, due to the complexities of professional politics, and that this failure had dashed his hopes of sustaining, in personal independence and with financial sufficiency, "the life that I live for you." Casting professional ambition and personal hopes aside, he would now turn his full attention back to the tragedy, which he expected to complete within a few months.[3] Hölderlin thus returned to *The Death of Empedocles* in the movement of a personal and decisive tragic turning.

Already in 1797, while serving as a live-in tutor to the Gontard family, Hölderlin sketched out a tragedy in five acts, focused on the figure of Empedocles. The Frankfurt Plan[4] shares with the three subsequent versions, all of which remained fragmentary, a guiding fascination with the philosopher's alleged self-immolation in the volcanic crater of Mt. Aetna.[5] Hölderlin does not understand this fatal leap as just a suicide, but as a quest for a union with Nature through the radiant, all-consuming, and purifying element of fire, which is always privileged in his poetics of the elements. The imperative to seek this union does not spring from chance events, but rather from Empedocles' inmost nature. Both his personal disposition and his philosophy incline him, according to Hölderlin (who shows here the influence of Rousseau), to disdain "culture" or civilization, which is integral to what he will later call "Art," and, still more fundamentally, to disdain all merely "one-sided" interests and engagements, simply because they restrict his devotion to the all, or to what he calls Nature. For this reason, even the most sensitive and beautiful of human relationships leave him dissatisfied and restless by their very singularity, or insofar as they are not experienced "in a great accord with all that lives," and also because he remains in thrall, through them, to time's "law of succession."[6] The temporality of experience, as well as the historicality of culture, despoil all such limited engagements in his eyes. One might indeed, on this basis, feel inclined to agree with Schürmann's charge that Hölderlin repudiates the singular. However, Wolfgang Riedel's erudite study of how, in the context of the history of ideas, Hölderlin came to write, around 1800, "the foundational texts of the 'modern' poetry [*Poesie*, which can also mean 'literature'] of union" (namely *Hyperion* and *The Death of Empedocles*) facilitates a deeper understanding. Riedel outlines the Neoplatonic (originally gnostic) quest for *henosis* (or union with the transcendent One from which the soul has become estranged) together with the quest's Christianization in patristic thought, and also in the mystical heritage of Pietism that formed Hölderlin's own natal religious milieu:

> The salvation of union is attained by sacrifice ('giving up'/*resignatio*) of the world (as well as of one's own self as belonging to the world). Here, in Christianity's most intensive pragmatics of salvation, the gnostic heritage asserts itself (as for Plotinus himself) as the foundational stratum of European religious history.[7]

Riedel goes on, however, to discuss the supplanting of this quest by the ideal of a return to and union with infinite nature and with the all of earthly life (which, of course, are not transcendent). He asks what enabled Hölderlin, about a century in advance of this turn in the history of ideas, "to change over the henotic discourse from *hen* [one] to *polla* [many], and to displace it from God unto nature;" and he answers (with Wegenast) in terms of the influence of Spinoza's understanding of God as nature, pointing to Hölderlin's 1790/91 notes on Jacobi's text on Spinoza.[8] However, although these notes (which are analytical rather than mystical) are interesting (not least for their reflections on Leibniz's debt to Spinoza), they cannot constitute a sufficient basis for elucidating Hölderlin's philosophy of nature in the Empedocles complex. Here one must supplement Riedel's analysis by considering Hölderlin's self-immersion in the actual thought of Empedocles (given especially that the Greek poets and thinkers remained his key intellectual and artistic guides).

To return, then, to the Frankfurt Plan, given Empedocles' dissatisfaction with all singular and limited relationships, it takes no more than a slight domestic misunderstanding—a passing cloud, as it were, in his relationship with his loving wife—and finally the unsurprising fickleness of popular acclaim, to impel him to seek a fiery death. Nevertheless, the very fact that such slight disturbances in human relationships (minor enough, in fact, to imperil the intended dramatic effect) can precipitate a momentous decision lends them, for all their supposed "one-sidedness," a gravity that is quite at odds with the protagonist's fundamental disdain for them. By their very nature, significant human relationships are unique; yet, even though Hölderlin here takes singularity to be restrictive, the weight he gives to such relationships sets the Frankfurt Plan apart from the three versions of *The Death of Empedocles*—even from the First Version, which richly develops the major characters' personalities and relationships to the protagonist. Hölderlin's fascination, as a poet, with the singular in its unique sensuous presencing, and his sensitivity to the nuances of human relationships, appear to be in tension here with his philosophical passion for effacing the singular in a union with Nature. What further distinguishes the three versions from the Frankfurt Plan is that in all of the former, but not in the Plan, Empedocles remains essentially solitary, a stranger to the human sphere, suggesting that Hölderlin may quickly have come to see his character's sensitivity to human bonds as imperiling his devotion to the all.

Empedocles, as Hölderlin portrays him, has enjoyed extraordinary powers, such as the power of healing, in virtue of his loving intimacy, cultivated since boyhood, with the elemental powers of Nature, referred to as the "genii of the world." Since, as he acknowledges, it is difficult for mortals to come to know these powers (which certainly have no Spinozan analogue) in their intrinsic and nonsubstantial purity (rather than merely in the familiar but degraded aspect of the material elements), he needed guidance in his youth, which he found human beings could not provide. He therefore entrusted himself directly and daringly to the sheer purity of light, or to the primordial radiance of manifestation. With the maturing of his spirit, which meant for him its increasing self-assimilation to light, he came to understand light's primordially pure nature and to allow this realization to shape his life: as well as to inform his poetic art. The following lines from the First Version are addressed to light itself:

And as you joyfully wander around mortals,
And, in heavenly youth, radiate forth gracious splendor
From yourself to each thing's own [being],
So that all wear your spirit's color—
Thus for me also life became a poem.[9]

He now modeled his own activity on that of light by giving himself, with unstinting generosity, to the "serious earth," heavy with its burden of destiny, in a range of beneficient activities empowered by his spiritual realization; and he found himself able to experience the joys of earthly life "as they are"—in their intrinsic being, which is to say, as fundamentally a play of "light" or energy, rather than in their ordinary gross and reified aspects. He found himself able to resolve the limitations of his individuality and finitude, as well as the enigmas that haunted him, in the depths of "ether" or pure space. His realization was also the source of his poetic song, which constituted his own offering to Nature.

To those unable to share his realization, he appeared to be possessed of mysterious and divine powers, and especially to be intimate with the secret life forces of "the beautiful world of plants," sprung forth from the interplay of the elements and nourished by light. Panthea, daughter of Kritias, the *archon* of Agrigentum (Akragas), whom he had miraculously restored to health when she was at the brink of death, by drawing on these very life forces, describes him as someone animated by "a fearsome, all-transforming life."[10]

Now, however, the grace of his spiritual realization, together with every power, has deserted him; and he feels himself abandoned, blinded, and cast into a desolation as profound as his earlier inspiration had been exalted. The tragic lapse (the *hamartia*) that brought about this alteration is one that Hölderlin describes, in a note, as integral to the hybristic exuberance of genius, the danger of which the ancients had a keen appreciation for whereas moderns do not fear it because they have become insensitive to it.[11] As Empedocles reflects, and as he explains to his baffled young disciple Pausanias, he allowed himself to be misled by the very simplicity and unfailing constancy of the elemental powers, and by his intimacy with them, into degrading and objectifying them while exalting his own person, as though Nature were at his command. In consequence, and in an exploitatation of popular acclaim and incomprehension, he hybristically declared himself a god.

Empedocles' untutored veneration of the sacredness of elemental Nature had long earned him the resentment of the priesthood, personified by the chief priest Hermokrates. Already as a boy, when he clung to sunlight and ether as "the messengers / Of great, distantly divined Nature," he felt, as he admits, a deep (and proto-Nietzschean) aversion to priests as cunning and hypocritical mercenaries of the sacred, as incapable of love, driven by resentment, and as the despoilers of any genuine inspiration.[12] Pausanias characterizes Hermokrates, with a striking allusion to the Grim Reaper, as felling Nature's youthful powers like meadow bloom cut down by the scythe.[13]

Hermokrates now seizes with vengeful cunning upon Empedocles' abjection. He not only incites Kritias and the people to banish him and places him under a curse, but he also seeks to deprive him of future communion with elemental Nature by proclaiming that the spring, the flame, the green and fruitful earth, the light, and the blessing of the air belong to the community and will not sustain one who is now excommunicated and consecrated "to the holy gods of death."

The primordial elements, however, cannot be possessed. Since Empedocles has dishonored and desacralized them—even if only, as Pausanias muses in bafflement, by a "mere word"—he must now purify himself and seek to unite himself anew with "all-forgiving Nature." However, unlike the initial, spontaneous union, a reunion in atonement demands his own sacrificial death, for "to mortals, nothing is granted for free."[14] What is granted to him, as soon as he forms his resolution to die (which he does in a flash of realization when he drinks of the limpid mountain stream) is the final blessing of the solar light, resplendent over "golden waters," the radiance of the constellations, the volcanic fire of earth, and the caress of "the all-moving, / The spirit, ether."[15] Although, as Kritias reflects, joy cannot be held fast by mortals, Empedocles finds joy at the threshold of death; and from the foaming "cup of terror" that Nature holds out to him, he will, as its poet, draw his last inspiration.[16] The fatal cup recalls, of course, Plato's account, in the *Phaedo*; of Socrates' imbibing the hemlock that brought him death; and Hölderlin (who had contemplated writing a tragedy on the death of Socrates) delineates here a Platonic inversion of the received valuations of life and death.

Life's passion and joy are finally kindled, for Empedocles, by death itself; and he, the votary of light, feels, on the verge of this "step into the dark," that he has only now begun truly to live. However, whereas Socrates disdains the body and is indifferent as to the disposal of his corpse,[17] Empedocles wants to give himself bodily to the deathless "holy spirit of the world," for which, since it is inherently and inalienably free, the body cannot be a prison. By leaping into the volcanic crater, he will merge his body with the fiery element, leaving no visible trace of its separate identity.[18] At the same time, this bodily merging with the life-and-death-granting power of Nature emphatically denies any aspiration to transcendence, to a surpassing of this world. This is a thought that Hölderlin will remain committed to even in his late philosophy of tragedy, and it is a thought that will ultimately allow him to cherish the singular, rather than to treat it, in Platonic fashion, as merely participating in a higher reality. Whereas Socrates, engaged in the philosophical "practice of dying," turns his back on the natural world, declaring that trees or the countryside have nothing to teach him,[19] Empedocles, the votary of Nature, exalts Nature even in his final words, which are addressed to the prismatic splendor of the rainbow:

> Oh bow of Iris above plunging
> Waters, when in silver clouds the wave
> Flies up, as you are, so is my joy.[20]

There are, to be sure, several further and inchoate strands of thought woven into Empedocles' justification of his suicide (which remains an important concern of the First Version): he cannot live at the ordinary level, deprived of "love and genius;" he will not leave this life ignominously in the decrepitude of old age or illness; the vessel that has held the spirit must be shattered, rather than left to the ravages of "self-will, and triviality, and dishonor;" and his sacrifice is that of "time's firstborn."[21] The last strand is important in that Hölderlin here, for the first time, suggests a link between Empedocles' sacrifical death and an imminent "turning of the times." With respect to the importance the question of time will generally have in Hölderlin's philosophy of tragedy, it may be relevant to consider here that, in his notes on Jacobi's *Letters* on Spinoza, he comments: "Lessing, moreover, shows him [Jacobi] a passage in Leibniz which is *obviously Spinozist*: there it is said of God [that] *he finds himself in an everlasting expansion and contraction. That would be the creation and the enduring of the world.*"[22]

Riedel traces the idea of divine expansion and contraction (which is not to be found in Spinoza) to the Kabbala and notes that it was influential, at the time of Hölderlin's writing, in heterodox Pietist circles. Its importance lies in "thinking the category time into the concept of God," and thus thinking God as process or (with Lessing) as "everlasting creation."[23] Empedocles, as "time's firstborn," would then sacrificially unite himself with the creative process or the temporality of manifestation (which is not here thought as conflictual). In the First Version, however, these lines of thought remain quite undeveloped and are neither integrated with each other nor with the the central theme of sacrificial conciliation.

The heart of the First Version is not Empedocles' death, but rather his final testament which, though long meditated on yet always hesitantly withheld, is now at last released to the people effortlessly, like a ripe fruit. This testament brings into focus what is at stake in the envisaged turning of the times. Every living being, Empedocles points out, must in death return to the elements which work unceasing transformation and renewal; but to humans alone it is given to do so freely—to enter into a symbolic "purifying death" by relinquishing all outworn forms of life. He therefore advocates a radical and creative forgetting of the established cultural, sociopolitical, and religious orders, admonishing the people to give themselves over to all-transforming

Nature rather than living out their lives in thrall to passive habituality and futility. If they do so, they will be able, as though newly born, to lift up their eyes to "divine Nature," their spirit kindled by heaven's light, and they will realize "deed and fame" from out of their communion with the primordial elements. Once they abandon the restricted perspective of worldly identities and preoccupations, and once their life, mindful of its origin, begins to unfold itself as a quest for "living beauty," they can at last hope to experience the advent of the gods. Enraptured by this vision, Empedocles exclaims ecstatically:

> It is they!
> The long-missed, the living,
> The good gods[24]

His vision, however, is not purely cosmic and religious, but also, and importantly, ethical, for it implies sociopolitical transformation. Firstly, once the elements, in their material manifestation, are honored in an awareness of their intrinsic sacrality, the entire relationship of humans to the natural world will be beneficially transformed. By realizing their genuine strength and wisdom, moreover, the people will at last become capable of self-determination, rather than being at the mercy of potentates, demagogues, or the priesthood. The new social order (inspired, for Hölderlin, by the guiding ideals of the French Revolution and by his reading of Rousseau) will institute full equality and community. Once this new order is realized, Empedocles feels assured, what is beautiful will no longer be stifled and die shut away in "a sadly silent breast." A figure such as he would then no longer lack human community.

The envisaged historical transformation does not depend on the continued presence and guidance of any particular individual, such as Empedocles himself (who otherwise could not justify his suicide), for Nature has no need of speech and once a glimpse of its intrinsic sacrality has been vouchsafed, it will, Hölderlin thinks, prove ineffaceable. Once people have realized this new consciousness, the blessing of the "heavenly fire" will ensoul all times to come; and the very constellations or the flowering earth will then bear witness and offer teachings.[25] This vision is quite obviously over-confident; and one must fear, as Hölderlin does not, that even what may be intrinsically ineffable may yet again become covered over and obscured, so that history can offer no pure instauration.

By the time Hölderlin began work on the Second Version in the spring of 1799, it had already become apparent that the South German revolutionaries, with whom he had been intimate through the mediation of his friend Isaac von Sinclair, not only could not count on any meaningful support from France, but had essentially been betrayed.[26] The Second Version reflects Hölderlin's political disenchantment in that Empedocles' transgression now no longer follows from the sheer exuberance of his solitary genius, but is rather a response to popular incomprehension and to his ensuing loneliness. The entire opening scene is occupied by an exchange between the priest Hermokrates and Mekades, cast here in place of Kritias as the *archon* of Akragas. Hermokrates now acknowledges both an underlying kinship and a disparity of power (in his own disfavor) between himself and Empedocles. He explains to Mekades that Empedocles had allowed himself to be blinded and misled by "the blind"—the uncomprehending populace to whom he had foolishly bared his soul—into accepting the poisoned solace of their adulation and divinization of his person out of an inability to bear his isolation:

> And names, such as I will not recount for you,
> The servants gave to the proud mourner,
> And finally the thirsty one accepts the poison,
> The unfortunate one, who does not know how to remain
> Alone with his thought [*Sinn*], and who finds nothing similar.[27]

In keeping with Hölderlin's elemental poetics of fire, Empedocles is now cast as a Promethean figure who, out of his excessive love for mortals (or perhaps his desire simply to connect with them), offered them "the heavenly flame of life," which they were unprepared to receive.[28] In doing so, he offended against the priestly code of secrecy and obscurantism, intended to safeguard priestly power (the power of the weak but cunning, as Nietzsche was to elaborate brilliantly), as well as against the institution of sovereignty, both of which operate at the cost of keeping the people from being nourished by the sheer energy of light and from entering into the living presence of the divine. More fundamentally, however, he also offended against divinity, which means, for him, the sacred elements, by telling the people that, even though they are always and everywhere sustained by "the free / Immortal powers of the world," their destinal condition of alienation has left them deprived and stunted, like wild-sown seedlings in inhospitable soil.[29] In a fast-moving meter (which contrasts with the stately hexameter of the First Version), Mekades recounts to Hermokrates that Empedocles then proclaimed that the vivifying power was his alone, and that he possessed it in virtue of *the poetic word*, which "names the unknown," and which can thus bring the elemental powers into harmonious relation, interconnecting the all with itself.[30] Thus, in the Second Version, Empedocles' self-divinization is based on an understanding of the poetic word as a power of naming and as a necessary supplement to Nature's powers. As Empedocles' satirical retrospective self-characterization highlights, he not only styled himself the lord and master of all cosmic powers, but he also dared to claim that divine spirit itself would be lifeless without the power of his word, which now no longer functions as his responsive offering to Nature, but as the supposed ground of Nature's very life:

> For what would heaven be, or the sea,
> Or islands and constellations, and all that lies
> Before the eyes of humans, what would they be,
> These dead playing strings, if I did not give them sound,
> And speech, and soul? What are
> The gods and their spirit, if I do not
> Announce them? Now, tell me, who am I?[31]

In having Empedocles characterize the poetic word as a power of naming, Hölderlin seems subtly to indicate the sclerosis that has afflicted him ever since the performance of his hybristic act; for, as Françoise Dastur points out, the name or noun (privileged in Greek thought) involves, as such, no reference to time.[32] If then the Empedocles of the First Version sought to unite himself with the temporality of manifestation, his hybristic exaltation of his own poetic genius as a power of naming has, in the Second Version, alienated him from Nature's temporality or process-character.

The fact that, in his self-accusation before his disciple Pausanias, the most insistently recurring words are the personal and possessive pronouns "I," "me," and "mine" probably points in the same direction. In a 1985 letter to Hegel, Hölderlin comments as follows on Fichte's absolute I:

> [It] contains all reality . . . there is therefore for this absolute I no object . . . but a consciousness without object is not thinkable; and if I myself am this object, then, as such, I am necessarily delimited, even if only as to time. . . . [T]hus in the absolute I no consciousness is thinkable; as absolute I, I have no consciousness, and insofar as I have no consciousness, I am (for myself) nothing; thus the absolute I is (for me) Nothing.[33]

In keeping with this reasoning, Empedocles, in seeking to absolutize his subjective consciousness (in the form of his power of naming), seeks to exempt himself from Nature's time-character (which would limit him). This act of self-aggrandization is not only hybristic, but ultimately nihilistic.

In the Second Version, Empedocles puts forward no final testament. His parting statement simply affirms that humans should act out of meditative calm, creatively furthering and gladdening the life that everywhere surrounds them. He now fully reintegrates his own gifts and "splendid . . . word" with the creative powers of Nature:

> Full of silent power encompasses
> Him who is aware—so that he may give form—the world,
> Great Nature,
> So that he may call forth
> Its spirit, man
> Carries care in his bosom, and hope[34]

Furthermore, in the Second Version, Empedocles himself no longer seeks to justify his decision to die. The justification is now offered only in retrospect by those who are spiritually closest to him: Panthea and his disciple Pausanias. Panthea reflects that those who fear death do not truly love Nature, whereas Empedocles died sacrificially, bearing witness to and uniting himself with the living and sacred All. Nature's sacred power, she muses, shows itself not merely in flower and fruit, but in transmuting suffering, so that, like Empedocles, life itself drinks its happiness from the chalice of death.[35] Although she acknowledges her grief, she does so with shame; for she must not cling to one whose deed was destinally fitting:

> So it had to happen,
> So spirit wants it
> And ripening time.[36]

Panthea's worshipful acquiescence, however, is insistently challenged by her Athenian guest-friend, Delia, who, in her devotion to life and the living, somewhat resembles Ismene in Sophocles' *Antigone*. Already in the First Version, Delia chides Panthea for loving Empedocles in a painful and self-sacrificial transport of adoration. She now remonstrates to her that what is truly beautiful is to dwell among humans, that her own heart finds repose therein, and that this earth remains magnificent and kindly. She finds Empedocles' self-chosen death distressingly incomprehensible, and she reproaches Pausanias for not having dissuaded him by the force of friendship. When Pausanias proclaims that Empedocles' genius flames up all the more brightly from his ashes, she counters that the hearts of mortals prefer a mild light and that mortals seek to fix their eyes on what is lasting.[37] She laments that the best, and the flower of youth, step over to the side of "the annihilating ones / The gods of death," making it seem shameful for others to want to live and dwell among mortals.[38]

However, whereas her similar lament in the First Version sounds the concluding tone of the tragedy (it is challenged only by a response from Pausanias which Hölderlin did not complete), in the Second Version her voice is almost drowned out by Panthea's and Pausanias's renewed glorification of Empedocles' death. She opposes what Hölderlin will later call "tragic transport" or "eccentric enthusiasm" with its passion for death (*Todeslust*); but her opposition, still vital in the First Version, is now not allowed to prevail; and in the Third Version, she will not even appear.

A key theme of the first two versions is the differential unity of Nature, and in particular the interrelation of the pure elemental energies. The importance of the primordial elements in the thought of *The Death of Empedocles* (particularly in the first two versions) and for Hölderlin's thought beyond the Empedocles corpus, has so far not been adequately recognized. As concerns the differential unity of Nature, Hölderlin had, in his epistolary novel *Hyperion*, similarly understood the Heraclitean ἕν διαφέρων ἑαυτῷ (the one differing from itself) as expressing the very essence of beauty (the source of both art and religion), and as the foundational word of philosophy. As Hyperion himself elaborates:

> The human being . . . who does not at least once in his life feel full and limpid beauty within himself . . . who has never experienced how, only in hours of inspiration, everything intimately agrees with itself, this human being will not even become a philosophical skeptic. . . . For, believe me, he who doubts finds contradiction and insufficiency in everything that is thought only because he knows the harmony of the flawless beauty which is never thought.[39]

Empedocles, for Hölderlin, resembles Hyperion in being a figure of "the dissolution of differences embodied in a specific character."[40] In his case, this dissolution is not due to what he, in the Preface to the "Fragment of *Hyperion*," calls the ideal of "highest *naïveté*," but rather to the opposed ideal of "highest self-cultivation [*Bildung*]."[41] The "eccentric path" that leads from the first ideal to the second promises to reach "the highest and most beautiful condition" that a human being can aspire to; but it also threatens to give free rein to "the dangerous side of man that craves everything, subjugates everything."[42] As a poet and philosopher (Hölderlin here understands poetry, in the wider sense of *Dichtung*, to be the precondition of philosophy),[43] Empedocles was able to reveal the self-differentiating unity of the all through the power of his artful speech; but in his hybristic lapse he gave way, if only briefly, to "the dangerous side of man" which estranged him from Nature.

The difficulty that, in the First and Second Versions, remains unresolved is that of showing in what way Empedocles' self-immolation is not only an act of atonement, but also, and even primarily, a genuine sacrificial offering, and further why such an offering should be needed to set on course an imminent historical transition. This difficulty may be the reason why Hölderlin abandoned the Second Version to undertake intricate and searching theoretical analyses focused on the philosophy of history as well as on issues in poetics before beginning work on the Third Version. A resolution of the difficulty will necessarily alter the dramatic structure of the tragedy so that it may find itself unable to conform to a classical paradigm such as that elaborated in Aristotle's *Poetics*. This can be seen in the virtual disappearance of plot in the Third Version, and it may bear on Hölderlin's abandoning his effort to write a modern tragedy based on Greek models. In considering the Third Version, then, it will also be necessary to work through a body of demanding essays.

THREE

Singularity and Reconciliation: The Third Version of *The Death of Empedocles*

> The tragic *poem*, *heroic in its external appearance*, is in its *fundamental tone* idealistic [*idealisch*]; and all works of this kind must be based on an intellectual intuition, which can be no other than that unity with all that lives, which . . . can be known by spirit.
>
> [F]or it is an eternal law that the whole, rich in content, does not feel itself in its unicity [*Einigkeit*] with that determinacy and liveliness . . . with which its parts . . . feel themselves, so that one can say that, when the liveliness, determinacy, and unity of the parts, wherein their wholeness is felt, transgresses the limits *of the latter* and becomes suffering and decisive separation [*Entschiedenheit*] and singularization as absolute *as possible*, then the *whole* feels itself *in these parts* . . .

Having abandoned the Second Version of *The Death of Empedocles* in late 1799, Hölderlin sought to work out his philosophy of tragedy and to clarify issues as to the poetics of tragedy in the essay now titled "Concerning the Tragic," which is comprised of three parts: a reflection on the tragic ode, the "General Ground," and the "Ground for Empedocles."[1] In manuscript, the "Plan for the Third Version" immediately follows these theoretical essays and is followed in turn by the Third Version itself, completed through act 1, scene 3.[2] The final text of the Empedocles complex, the "Project for the Continuation of the Third Version," is preceded by a further theoretical essay, "The Fatherland in Decline" ("Das untergehende Vaterland"), which sets forth a philosophy of history and brings it into relation to the poetics of tragic presentation (*Darstellung*).[3]

Hölderlin's opening reflections on the tragic ode in "Concerning the Tragic" are evidently connected with his introduction of a tragic chorus in the Third Version.[4] In early 1800, he translated extensively from Pindar's Olympian and Pythian Odes;[5] and his discussion here not only reflects the tone of the Pindaric ode (which has been characterized as "emotional, exalted, and intense"),[6] but also seeks to bring the latter's tripartite schema of strophe, antistrophe, and epode into conjunction with a tripartite dialectical structure. Given that, in the Third Version, all decisions and actions lie in the past, so that, in violation of the principles of Aristotle's *Poetics*, plot loses its importance, Hölderlin may also have felt the need to secure the dramatic character of the tragedy by setting apart the tragic ode, recited by the chorus, from the lyric ode.

The tragic ode begins, according to Hölderlin, in the searing intensity of "highest fire;" it attests to spirit's transgression of limits in life-involvements which tend, of themselves, toward contact or engagement. Hölderlin here names consciousness, reflective thought (*Nachdenken*), and bodily sensuousness. What the ode, in its reflection on transgressive engagements, seeks to achieve is the presentation (*Darstellung*) of what is "pure;" and its path toward this goal is dialectical. The conflict that results from an intial excess of intensity (*Innigkeit*) is presented in fictive form; and this fictive distancing allows for both decisive differentiation (*krisis*) and need (*Not*) to come to word. By the mediacy of a "natural act" (which Hölderlin does not specify further), the ode finds itself propelled onward to the opposed extreme of "a non-differentiation of the pure, the trans-sensory, which seems to acknowledge no need whatever."[7] It then achieves a reconciliation of the opposed extremes and comes to rest in a tone of quieted reflection, or in purified sensuousness. Although this new tone proves too modest and subdued for a tragic ending, it allows the initial intensity to be now experienced, as if from a certain distance, and as an extreme. And out of this "experience and recognition of heterogeneity," the ode can at last reflectively return to its original, exalted tone. Furthermore, the ideality that already interlinked the two extremes (of discriminating intensity and transcendent nondifferentiation) can now be made manifest as such in its purity.

In the "General Ground," Hölderlin reflects, however, that tragic drama as a whole expresses "deepest intensity" in a different manner than does the tragic ode; for, whereas the latter presents it with immediacy and in the forms of feeling, the former resorts, in its proper mode of presentation (*Darstellung*), to a certain veiling, necessitated by the fact that what it brings to expression is "more infinitely divine." There is here no personal immediacy or urgency; and, even though the tragic poet must write from out of his own life-experience and, indeed, his very soul, subjectivity is not foregrounded. Rather, the poet transposes his experience of the divine, gained within his own life-world, unto "alien, analogical material," which thus takes on a symbolic character.[8] The more the intensity that is brought to expression approaches transgression or *nefas*,[9] the greater the need to set apart the actual human being, together with his or her sensibility, from the "felt element," so as to restrain the rush of feeling (what will later be termed "tragic transport") within firm bounds. The remote and alien character of the material (as was the legendary death of Empedocles in Germany at the threshold of the 19th century), as well as the severity and separative force of the form (Hölderlin will later emphasize the importance of the interrupting *caesura*), serve to bring about the needed restraint.

The veiling thus effected must nonetheless remain transparent if the drama is to have vitality and meaning. The divine, such as the poet has experienced it in his own life-world, must not be allowed to become obscured or negated by the alien context. Thus, in tragic drama (which, for Hölderlin, expresses a deeper intensity than lyric poetry), a difficult balance must be maintained between a relinquishment of subjectivity and of personal passions (which are ephemeral), and a "preservation" of the felt intensity that these made possible within an "alien vessel," as though the life-intensity had alchemically been transmuted into an elixir, a transtemporal, hieratic form.

In "pure life" (perhaps that of Homeric Greece), Nature and Art, according to the "Ground for Empedocles," oppose one another "only harmoniously," in a relationship of complementarity. Art, together with the inspired skill and the conceptual ordering that enable its creation, is the very flower of Nature, whereas Nature becomes, through Art, the bearer of perfection, so that the divine reveals itself "in the midst of both."[10]

This complementarity, however, can be grasped only by feeling. Intellectual apprehension requires presentation (*Darstellung*), which in turn presupposes clear differentiation. The excessive intensity that brought about the harmonious merging of opposites must therefore be purified by separation. "Organic" (individuated) man must now assert his autonomous agency through consciousness, art, and reflection, whereas "aorgic" (unformed) Nature must show itself as refractory to human feeling, comprehension, or delimitation.[11] Through ongoing differentiation, the opposites are now once again brought face to face; but Nature has become more organic through the influence of the formative forces of culture, or *Bildung*, whereas humans, exposed to the influence of aorgic Nature, have become more open to the unlimited or infinite. Hölderlin stresses that the feeling that now apprehends the opposites together and at one, not in undifferentiated unity, but rather in their differentiation, "belongs, perhaps, to the highest that can be felt."[12] Not only has a dialectical progression occurred, so that the interrelation of the organic and aorgic principles has become richer or "more infinite," but human beings, whose initial organicism has been enlivened, inspired, and given a vaster visionary scope by the aorgic principle, and aorgic Nature itself, which has in contrast taken on an (organic) pleasing form (*Wohlgestalt*), are brought together in an interrelation that leaves to each its distinctness.

Whereas the divine lay in the midst of the initial harmonious opposition, what lies in the midst, or at the chiasmatic intersection, of the new differential union is "the death of the singular." This death occurs because the organic extreme is driven to tear itself more and more away from its own "midpoint" in clinging to the aorgic, which it seeks to individualize (this is perhaps the new, and more danger-fraught sense now given to the human being's relationship to the primordial elements), whereas the aorgic extreme is driven to concentrate itself into a midpoint, so that both are alienated from their essentiality. Although, through this mutual self-alienation, a certain reconciliation has been achieved in that the organic extreme seems to return to itself by individualizing the aorgic while the aorgic extreme seems similarly to incorporate the organic by taking on form, this reconciliation can only be momentary. Hölderlin stresses that it is indeed so fleeting as to approach illusion; for the energies of the opposed powers continue immediately to affect and disintegrate it:

> *But the individuality of this moment is only a product of highest strife, its generality only a product of highest strife.* Thus, when reconciliation appears to be there, and the organic again influences this moment in its own manner, and the aorgic [also] in its own, then, due to the impressions of the organic, the aorgically originated individuality contained in this moment becomes again more aorgic. Due to the impressions of the aorgic, the organically originated generality contained in this moment becomes again more particular, so that the uniting moment dissolves like a phantom . . .[13]

The death of the singular (which has so far been characterized only abstractly, as the disintegration of the fleeting moment of reconciliation) is not, however, a sheer loss. In keeping with the German Idealist schema of transmuting loss into spiritual gain, it is the sacrificial cost of a "more beautiful" and stable reconciliation yet to be achieved. The deceptive aspect of the union, which was due to its being "too intense" by virtue of its being brought about in sheer singularity (in the person of a visionary such as Empedocles), has now been overcome; and the divine no longer manifests itself in concrete, sensuous form. Rather, the organic extreme now shows itself in a purified generality, and the aorgic as an object of calm contemplation, so that the two can at last be apprehended in their interrelation yet without any loss of differential clarity.

The destiny of Empedocles is played out in the context of this epochal drama of opposition and reconciliation.[14] Born into an age marked by the extreme antagonism between Art and Nature, and as a man of high gifts and consuming intensity, he sought to reconcile and unite the warring extremes *in his own person*, thus allowing the conciliating moment to become sensuously singular and concrete. He succeeded so remarkably that, in his own creativity and intelligence, the principial antagonism was effaced, leading to an unprecedented and irrepeatable amalgamation and inversion of the opposites. Intellectual analysis and organization did not, for him, spring from his own subjectivity; rather, what was unformed, general, and unconscious appeared to him quite spontaneously to take on form, specificity, and consciousness. Conversely, within his own psychological subjectivity, he embraced what is formless, incomprehensible, and incomparable, so that it ceased thereby to be a merely "objective" given or surd. Thus, he became, in Hölderlin's terms, more aorgic in his own individuality while giving organic form and articulate voice to what otherwise aorgically repudiates thought and speech.

Hölderlin recognizes not only the decisive role of epochal historicity, but also the influence of geographic locality in the formation of Empedocles' character and tragic destiny. He was a son both of "his heaven and his period," in sum, of his "native land," so that he first encountered the aorgic element, which he strove to bring to an intellectually and poetically ordered (organic) presentation, in the radiant exuberance of Sicilian nature. Conversely, the bold, inventive "art spirit" characteristic of his people was intensified in him to the point of becoming aorgically encompassing and unlimited. Similarly, his drive to accomplish sociopolitical innovation magnified (on the side of Art) the hyper-political engagement and inventiveness characteristic of his people, but he equally embodied (on the side of Nature) their anarchic spirit of independence and self-sufficiency.

The unification of the opposed principles in his own person, or in his concrete and sensuous singularity, meant that they appeared to pass seamlessly into one another, in an ardent intimacy (*Innigkeit*) that was excessive precisely because it effaced all customary differentiation. This union, however, was also inherently deceptive and unstable since it expressed, if only in a masked way, the extremity of strife:

> [T]his *real excess of ardent intensity* arises out of hostility and highest strife, where the aorgic takes on the humble aspect of the particular—thus appearing to reconcile itself with the over[ly]-organic—[and] the organic takes on the humble aspect of the general—thus appearing to reconcile itself with the over[ly]-aorgic, over[ly]-living—[only] because the two interpenetrate each other most deeply at the highest extremity, and therewith must take on, in their outer form, the aspect and semblance of their opposites.[15]

Empedocles, "born to be a poet" (Hölderlin, as poet and thinker, casts him perhaps in his own image), was suited to bring about this deceptive and fleeting unification because he tended, in his very subjectivity (his organic aspect), to envisage the encompassing whole, whereas he conversely inclined to express even his own passional nature (his aorgic aspect) in lucid images and forms. The interpenetration of the two contrary energies (which may prefigure Nietzsche's two art impulses inherent in nature)[16] was thus prepared for by his high poetic gifts. However, he was unable to consummate these gifts within their proper sphere and in the restraint and purity that would have allowed the attunement (*Stimmung*) thus brought to expression to give direction to his people (as had been Homer's privilege); for the destiny of his time called for neither song nor deed, but for sacrifice:

> [I]t [the destiny of the time] demanded a *sacrifice*, the entire human being, who becomes really and visibly that, wherein the destiny of his time seems to resolve itself, wherein the extremes seem to unite themselves really and visibly as one . . . must perish, because in him the sensible [*sinnliche*] unification, born out of need and strife in advance of its time, showed itself and seemed to resolve the problem of destiny, which, however, cannot ever resolve itself visibly and individually . . ."[17]

If it could thus resolve itself, Hölderlin reflects, the dynamic life of an entire world-order would die away in singularity. In "Concerning the Tragic," the hybristic moment is no longer a personal transgression, but rather an individual's destinally provoked attempt to reconcile the opposed principles of Nature and Art in his or her sheer singularity. The tragedy now revolves upon the destinal role and sacrifice of the singular in the face of the antagonistic principles that are hostile to singularity. The aorgic principle effaces singularity by in-different unification and the organic by a subsumptive ordering which recognizes only the particular. In the Empedocles complex, Hölderlin is not (as Schürmann charges) hostile to singularity; rather, the singular individual becomes, for him, a sacrificial and tragic figure insofar as he or she seeks heroically to resolve a given historical modality of the conflict at the core of manifestation by reconciling the warring principles in his or her own person. It still remains to be seen, however, how Hölderlin will understand tragic singularization in his translations and interpetations of Sophoclean tragedy.

In the First and Second Versions, Empedocles' intimacy with the primordial elements of Nature alienated him from his people, who viewed him at best with incomprehension and at worst with hostility. His effort to master Nature was presented as a hybristic transgression, a betrayal of his intimate reciprocity with the primordial elements. Now, however, he is a still more Promethean figure who shares in and carries to an extreme the "free-spirited boldness" of his people, who refuse to recognize anything refractory to human comprehension and agency. For this reason (rather than out of personal *hybris*) he seeks to understand Nature and to subdue the overpowering influence of "the element" (this term, now used mostly in the singular, has come to stand for aorgic Nature). He cannot do so, however, without also assimilating himself to the element, thus tearing himself away from his own "midpoint," his stability as an individual. The aorgic element now manifests its ambiguous aspect: although it may appear welcoming and life-sustaining, it is an alien and unfathomable power that—for all the effort to conceal it behind the screens of cultural and intellectual constructs—fatally attracts sensitive individuals. Somewhat like the Freudian death drive, it impels the individual toward dissolution or a return to the unformed.

Hölderlin relates the aorgic element to the unconscious (or, perhaps, nonconscious) dynamics of the psyche, which means that it now infiltrates the supposed organicism of subjectivity, eroding its boundaries and affecting it with alterity. Empedocles' sensitivity and openness to these dimensions of the psyche enabled him to seek a reconciliation of Art with Nature at the very point where, to his people, Nature seemed most refractory to Art.[18] The people would have preferred to mask or ignore these dynamics; and they are repelled rather than charmed by a representation that gives them artistic form. Empedocles' priestly opponent seizes hold of this resistance, and thus, Hölderlin writes, "the fable unfolds."

The figure of the priest is drawn far more sympathetically in the Third Version and in the theoretical analyses that prepare for it than was the case in the earlier versions. He is now characterized as highly gifted, as the equal of Empedocles, and as heroic by nature. Some of his traits suggest perhaps the intellectual personality of Hegel, who was, of course, Hölderlin's friend from their student days at the Tübinger Stift, and whom he had helped, in 1797, to find a position as live-in tutor (*Hauslehrer*) in Frankfurt, close to himself.[19] Shortly after Hegel's arrival (in January 1779), Hölderlin wrote to his friend Christian Ludwig Neuffer that having contact with Hegel was beneficial to himself since "calm people of reason" can provide one with orientation in life's complexities.[20] In "Concerning the Tragic," he characterizes Empedocles' priestly opponent as someone whose virtue is reason, and whose goddess necessity:

> He is destiny itself, only with the difference that the warring forces are, within him, tied fast to a consciousness, to a point of separation, which keeps them clearly and securely opposed, [and] which fastens them to a (negative) ideality and gives them a direction.[21]

Unlike Empedocles, he does not so much strive to unite the warring extremes as to restrain them, connecting their interaction to "something abiding and firm" that is posited between them and that keeps both within their limits. Nevertheless, insofar as, for this opponent, creative action is essentially conceptual and so takes on the form of objectivity, whereas his subjectivity asserts itself in the "passive" form of firm endurance and calm abiding, he, in his own way, brings the opposed principles to exchange form and thus unites them.

Hölderlin, who had written, probably in 1796, an exquisite translation of Hekabe's (Hecuba's) pleading with Agamemnon for the life of her daughter in Euripides' *Hecuba*,[22] opens the Third Version in a manner reminiscent of that tragedy (which opens with the monologue of a child's ghost), with a soliloquy by Empedocles, who has already consecrated himself to death. Now that Mt. Aetna is offering him the fiery chalice, "filled with spirit to the brim," he feels himself divested of all human cares or bonds, light and buoyant as though capable of flight.[23] He has, to be sure, been treated unjustly and inhumanely; but the "poison" of this treatment on the part of his own brother, Strato (here the ruler of Agrigentum), and also of the people, serves him (in the ambiguous manner of *pharmaka*) as a medicine to cure his own "sin" of never having "loved humans humanly." He has served them well, to be sure, but without either passion or tenderness, just as the primordial elements of water and fire impartially sustain life. In death, he will now return to what is truly his own, to Nature's maternal embrace; and he invokes, in particular, "the magical, terrible flame" that, as a "bound spirit," is "the soul of what lives" yet is equally the bringer of death.[24]

The human love of which he was incapable is, however, extended to him by his young friend and disciple Pausanias. Pausanias has found, for him who is drawn to the flame and to high ether, a more grounding sacred and elemental abode: a deep cave, situated close to a spring, its entrance shaded by health-giving vegetation. To the radiant and consuming flame of Empedocles' "secret desire"—a symbol of aorgic passion—he opposes the solidity, abundance, and sheltering darkness of earth. The womblike cave could also be read as a figure of natality, which counteracts Empedocles' infatuation with death. Given his own aorgically inspired vision, however, and his need to sever all human bonds, Empedocles seeks above all to release Pausanias from his intense attachment to and love for himself, his mentor and teacher:

> Look up and dare! What one thing is breaks asunder;
> Love does not die in its bud,
> And everywhere in free joy
> Life's lofty tree shares itself out.[25]

Although he is moved and briefly tempted by Pausanias's willingness to follow him even into the abyss, he rejects the Platonic ideal of a "festive pair" of friends departing life together.[26] No temporal bond can endure and, in particular, his destiny is not to be shared. He counsels Pausanias to travel alone on to Italy, and from there to Greece, to visit Plato, the friend of his youth, by the "flowery Ilissus," and finally, should his soul still be restless, to visit also "the brothers in Egypt" who are concerned with astronomy and with "the book of destiny." His parting admonition to Pausanias foreshadows Nietzsche's thought of eternal return:

> Go, fear nothing! All things return;
> And what is to come to pass is already accomplished.[27]

The issue of a historically mandated tragic destiny, which is central to "Concerning the Tragic," does not come into focus in Empedocles' soliloquy nor in his exchange with Pausanias. The key themes sounded here are rather, as in the earlier versions, Empedocles' intimacy with the pure elements (among which fire has now become the emblem of the aorgic power), together with the tension between his essential solitude and the depth and power of human love. In the third and final (completed) scene, however, Empedocles is challenged critically to examine and justify his destinal and sacrificial role by the Egyptian priest and seer Manes.

Manes hints at an ancient bond, forged in Egypt, between Empedocles and himself (in keeping with Empedocles' own earlier reference to "the brothers in Egypt"). The indication (in lines 329–334) is that he is, in fact, no longer among the living but spectrally manifests himself since Empedocles has need of "a word." Although Manes does not seek to dissuade Empedocles from his suicidal decision as such (for mortals, he holds, are free to choose their death), he admonishes him that to embrace a sacrificial death at this crucial historical moment is the mandate and privilege of only a single One, and not of every emotional Greek who may feel called to it. The Christlike "new savior" to come, Manes acknowledges, is greater than himself. As one "born of light and night," he will stir up tumult and feud, given the critical configuration of the times; but he is ultimately a bringer of reconciliation. Above all, he will reconcile humans with the gods, healing their mutual estrangement, so that both can live "close [to each other] again, as of old."[28] Since the sacred spirit of life must not be held captive by any singular being, however, this savior will not glory in and seek to maintain his own separate identity. On the contrary, he will deliberately shatter his own happiness and even bring about his undoing so that, having purified whatever he had called his own, he will then restore it to "the element that glorified him." Manes's burning question is whether Empedocles is indeed this messianic awaited One, rather than someone who, however gifted and accomplished, is only pursuing a personal and misguided passion.

Empedocles, although vexed at being interrogated and challenged at the threshold of death, feels compelled to respond. He recounts how, already as a boy, he was enraptured by "the great figures of this world," the divine elements or elemental divinities. He was moved spontaneously to poetry or poetic prayer in which he named these "gods of Nature;" and he felt able to resolve life's enigmas intuitively through the radiant word or image, rather than by conceptual thought. Yet the tumult of his time did not allow him to live his life in the manner natural to him, in contemplation and artistic pursuits, cultivating his natal gifts, but ignoring the desperate "voice of the people," and the strife, suffering, and alienation that everywhere surrounded him. Recognizing in these phenomena the mark of divine abandonment ("the parting god of the people"), he took it upon himself to bring about a reconciliation. Amidst the blessings that ensued, and the gratitude and veneration that the people lavished upon him, however, a new and somber realization dawned:

> For, when a country is to die away, spirit chooses
> A single One for itself in the end, through whom
> Its swan song, the last life, resounds.[29]

He understood now that he was this chosen One, that the reconciliation he had brought about was a mirage that could not endure, and that the time had come to offer himself to spirit and to the pure elements in death.

Although he had not allowed Pausanias to join him in death, he invites Manes to this ultimate communion; yet he immediately checks himself, realizing that, for the seer, to do so is "forbidden fruit."[30] His autobiographical narrative has assured Manes that he is indeed the chosen One who is to consummate the turning of the times, or to inaugurate a new epochal configuration, by his self-sacrifice. His response to Manes has merged the theme of the pure elements, as developed in the earlier versions, with the messianic paradigm of a destinal reconciliation achieved through the sacrifice of the singular "chosen One." With respect to both of these thought-complexes, Hölderlin's focus remains trained on reconciliation and sacrifice. In this respect, his interpretation of tragedy in the Empedocles complex is congruent with Hegel's (for whom, moreover, the absolute itself is tragic and organized by a logic of sacrifice in its very unfolding). De Beistegui's comments on Hegel are equally pertinent to Hölderlin's thought in the Empedocles complex:

> By subordinating tragic action to the necessity of its reconciliation, Hegel turns dramatic representation into the figurative expression of the speculative, the prefiguration of the philosophical and of history as the "site" or "stage" of the reconciliation of Spirit immersed in its negativity.[31]

In the Third Version, the logic of an essential sacrifice is so insistent that no restraining voice, such as the voice of Delia in the earlier versions, can any longer be heard; it is a question only of the legitimation of Empedocles' self-sacrifice. Not only does Delia no longer appear, but there is, strikingly, not a single female character who participates in the tragic action or in its interpretation, which unfold entirely as an interchange among men. Panthea, to be sure, is mentioned in the Plan and also appears in the Third Version's list of characters; but she has no voice in the completed portion of the drama. Interestingly, in the cast of characters, she appears now as the *sister* of Empedocles, recalling Hegel's privileging of the figure of the sister. The male characters themselves are presented more as idealized figures than as concrete individuals. The Third Version thus neglects character development as well as plot; and dramatic structure has given way to the formulation of philosophical thought in exalted poetic diction. One suspects that, in Hölderlin's amalgamation of Greek mythical, tragic, and philosophical motifs with a Judeo-Christian logic of sacrifice (recalling the sacrifice demanded of Abraham, as well as that of Christ), the ancient philosopher-poet and visionary Empedocles is called upon to bear a speculative burden that he can hardly sustain.

Faced with the challenge of carrying the tragedy forward, notwithstanding its dramatic depletion, and the difficulty of showing how Empedocles' self-sacrifice can function as the pivot, so to speak, of a momentous epochal transition, Hölderlin undertook a philosophical exploration of historical process and of its tragic presentation (*Darstellung*) in the essay "Das untergehende Vaterland" ("The Fatherland in Decline"), also known as "Das Werden im Vergehen," or "Becoming in Perishing."[32] The essay is conceptually intricate and linguistically dense, partly due to Hölderlin's use of complex terminological inversions (such as "ideally individual" versus "individually ideal"), but more fundamentally due to the fact that the text was, as a working paper, not intended for readers other than himself.

Whereas, in the Frankfurt Plan, Hölderlin had his protagonist, Empedocles, reject everything singular, together with the temporality of experience, as being "one-sided" and therefore unsatisfactory, he now argues that "the all in all things" can present itself (*sich darstellen*) only in and through the temporality of historical process, marked by the emergence and decline of singular world-configurations. He compares historicity to language, on the grounds that both always bring to expression or to self-presentation "a living but singular whole."[33]

The declining "fatherland" is not a *patria* in the patriotic sense, but a world-configuration (involving both human life and Nature in their intimate interrelation) that constitutes one's inherited and accepted framework of meaning. In the entropic process of its disintegration, it can no longer open up vistas for or validate decisions and courses of action. For this reason, and because, in a context of epochal disintegration, one may have to confront incompatible obligations, or what Schürmann calls "ultimate double binds,"[34] the decline of the "fatherland" is a time of tragedy.

Hölderlin's focus, however, remains trained on emergence and innovation, and on the open horizon of possibility, rather than on conflict and dissolution as such. One cannot, he points out, even feel or experience pure dissolution; rather, the possible that gains reality at the point of dissolution is what is efficacious (*wirkt*) and what also allows for feeling and for recollection (*Erinnerung*), that is, for the modality in which the past, in its very dissolution, becomes an "ideal object." Recollection of the dissolved singular reintegrates it into "the infinite feeling of life;" and the process of "ideal dissolution" is everywhere also one of creation. Each of its points is "infinitely" interrelated with every other point as well as with the "total feeling" (the feeling of life).[35]

Tragic drama, or "genuine tragic language," therefore does not bring to expression sheer, incomprehensible misfortune, anguish, or pain (which would, in Aristotelian terms, evoke only the *unpurified* passions of terror and pity). Insofar as it gives expression to horror and agony, it does so "through what is harmonious, comprehensible, [and] living," so that at the origin of genuine tragic language lies "the ever creative." What is at work here, he concludes, is "a heavenly fire rather than an earthly one," so that one witnesses, not sheer destruction and sorrow, but a limitless interpenetration of pain and joy, conflict and peace, or form and the formless. In such "idealistic dissolution" (*idealische Auflösung*), and in its tragic presentation, there is neither fear nor stagnation; it follows, instead, its own unerring trajectory:

> [It] freely and completely passes through the singular point in all its interrelations with the remaining points of dissolution and of bringing-about [*Herstellung*], which lie in between the two initial points *capable* of dissolution and of bringing-about, namely those that lie in between the opposed infinitely new and the finitely old, the really total and the ideally particular.[36]

In contrast to the philosophical understanding and tragic presentation of idealistic dissolution, a preoccupation with "so-called real dissolution" tends to fixate only on loss and to recoil from it as from sheer negativity. Here, the existing order, or the singular which happens to obtain (*jedes Bestehende also Besondere*) is maximized and presents itself as the "all," so that an understanding out of touch with idealistic dissolution is easily misled into totalization. If the dissolution of the "ideally individual" is grasped in its true character, however, it does not show itself as a weakening and as death, but as vivification and growth; and even the dissolution of the "infinitely new" will not attest to annihilating violence, but rather to "love." Both moments of dissolution together constitute "a (transcendental) creative act" that unites the ideally individual with what is really infinite.[37]

This union or reconciliation constitutes the spiritual work of tragedy and it gives tragedy its dignified calm; for, once the "infinitely real" and the "finitely ideal" are reconciled and no longer harshly opposed, transition, or becoming and passing away, lose their power to agitate. Every new configuration that comes into being will, to be sure, still seek to assert and maximize itself; but it encounters its epochal limits once the "infinitely new" (as the open horizon of creativity and possibility) is experienced, in its relation to the merely "individually new," as an alien and destructive power.

For Hölderlin, the idealistic vision of tragic dissolution is one that sees the singular (or "the part," in the terminology of "On the Difference of Poetic Modes")[38] as reconciled with the whole in the extremity of its isolation and in its very undoing; for the unity of the whole is dynamic and differential. As such it demands, but also desolates, the most "lively" self-assertion of singularities. Jean-François Courtine interprets this thought in terms of Hölderlin's intellectual relation to Fichte and Schelling:

> Against Fichte and Schelling, Hölderlin is seeking here [in the essay fragment "Urteil und Sein"] to distinguish being as such, insofar as it is expressed in intellectual intuition, from the putatively immediate identity revealed in the affirmation of the I by itself, in its absolute self positing. . . . It is when the parts are most thoroughly differentiated and dissociated, and are no longer anything but parts, that, paradoxically, unity is most determinate. Or again: unity, the "primordially united," only appears at the extreme limit of partition . . .[39]

Given, then, that the unitariness (*Einigkeit*) of the whole, which Hölderlin seeks to bring to tragic presentation or *Darstellung*, is without any closure or completion and is manifest only as *archē*-partition, or as the agonal temporal spacing of singularities, he distances himself from any self-absolutizing "hegemonic phantasm," such as the One, subjectivity, or even spirit. The living and therefore conflictual unicity of the whole repudiates any *archē*. In this undercutting of any governing principle in the historical process, one can perhaps trace the root of Hölderlin's eventual deconstruction of the speculative matrix of tragedy, which he had himself striven to elaborate[40]—a dismantling that will, however, be consummated only in his late translations and interpretations of two of Sophocles' Theban tragedies.

Any singular world-configuration or epochal "new world" must yield to a quasi-Anaximandrian *taxis* of time, to be preserved only in the ideality of interiorizing remembrance. Although, in the "Project for the Continuation of the Third Version,"[41] Hölderlin wants Manes to recognize, in Empedocles, "the chosen one who would kill and give life, in whom and through whom a world at once disintegrates and renews itself," "The Fatherland in Decline" ignores the sacrificial role of Empedocles as an exceptional individual. Here, there seems, for the first time in Hölderlin's thought on history and the tragic, to be no longer any need for or consequent justification of such a destinal role or for a sacrifice that would be essential for accomplishing a reconciliation within history. Thus, the philosophical understanding of tragedy that inspired *The Death of Empedocles* finds itself driven, at last, to self-questioning. At the same time, as already noted, the philosophical burden that, for Hölderlin, the tragedy had to bear endangered its dramatic viability. The very liveliness and self-assertion of the singular that he emphasizes in "The Fatherland in Decline" begins to elude him in the context of the dramatic presentation of the tragic characters and their interaction. Hölderlin abandoned work on *The Death of Empedocles* and did not return to the philosophy and poetics of tragedy until his Sophocles translations. Although only about three years separate the two bodies of work, for Hölderlin, this interval of time brought with it major transitions in his life and thought.

FOUR

Between Hölderlin's Empedocles and Empedocles of Akragas

> But come, if the form of my previous arguments was in any way incomplete, take note of the witness of these to what I have said before: the sun, white[-hot] to behold and hot throughout, heavenly bodies drenched in heat and shining light, rain everywhere dark and chill; and from the earth issue forth things firmly rooted and solid. Under anger, they have different forms and are all separate; but under affection, they come together and desire one another. From these come all the things that were and are and will be—trees spring up, and men and women, and [land] animals, and birds, and water-nourished fish, and the long-lived gods, highest in honor. For these [elements] alone are real; and as they run through one another, they take on different forms; for their intermingling changes them.

Although Hölderlin relied mainly on Diogenes Laërtius's account of Empedocles' life and thought, without benefit of critical scholarship,[1] his dramatization is both erudite and philosophically insightful. Given his own strongly held democratic (or, in the terminology of his time, "republican") and egalitarian political ideals (notably as they inspired the French Revolution), he shows himself particularly impressed by the biographical tradition concerning Empedocles' refusal of the kingship of Akragas offered to him, given that he was a champion of freedom and adverse to sovereignty of any kind, and by the story, passed from Neanthes to Diogenes Laërtius, that when tyranny was about to take hold of the city, Empedocles persuaded the citizens to set aside their controversies so as to be able to espouse a democratic form of government.[2] Hölderlin draws on this narrative tradition in the final testament that he puts into the mouth of Empedocles in the First Version. He also incorporates other details from the biographical tradition, as preserved by Diogenes Laërtius, ranging from the confusion, prevalent in antiquity, between Empedocles himself and his grandfather, purportedly of the same name, who won an Olympic horse race in 496 B.C.E. (Hölderlin's Delia ascribes this victory to Empedocles the philosopher), on to his healing of a desperately ill woman named Pantheia (Panthea). However, what is for Hölderlin the key element of that tradition, Empedocles' supposed leap into Mt. Aetna's crater, is today considered apocryphal. Even Diogenes Laërtius mentions it only as one of several different narratives concerning Empedocles' death. Contemporary scholarship traces the story to Heraclides Ponticus and rejects it, not only on scholarly grounds, but also on the basis of geographical near-impossibility.[3]

Hölderlin, however, did not just draw on biography, but was deeply inspired by Empedocles' thought; and it is also striking that elements of Empedoclean diction still resonate in his late hymn *Andenken*, where the penultimate verse, "Und die Lieb' auch heftet fleissig die Augen" ("And love also diligently fixes its eyes") echoes Empedocles' Fragment 86:

> Ἐξ ὧν ὄμματ' ἐπήξεν ἀτείρεα δῖ' Ἀφροδίτη
>
> Out of these [elements] divine Aphrodite fashioned untiring eyes.[4]

With respect to Hölderlin's tragic figure of Empedocles, however, the two main interconnections between his own thought and that of the pre-Socratic philosopher concern the ontological primacy and sacredness of the elements, together with the two opposed cosmic forces of Love and Strife that agitate them, and the fall, suffering, and redemption of the spirit or *daimōn* consequent upon a transgression. These themes are crucial, respectively, to Empedocles' two philosophical poems, *On Nature* (*Περὶ φύσεως*) and *Purifications* (***Καθαρμοί***); and they will need to be traced out here for the sake of gaining a comparative perspective.

Empedocles addresses "On Nature" to his disciple Pausanias, son of Anchites, whom he exhorts to devote, not only his detached intellect, but also all his senses to attaining the full range of understanding that the mind of a mortal can aspire to. The pithy statement in Fragment 17 that "learning will increase your understanding" certainly remains a timeless instructional motto. Understanding, however, is not just an end in itself for Empedocles, but rather, in *On Nature*, it is also the pathway to acquiring beneficient powers. In Fragment 111, Pausanias is promised not only the ability to control the climate as well as knowledge of medicines to counteract illnesses and the ravages of old age, but even the ability to "bring out of Hades a dead man restored to strength." As Jean Bollack points out, this fragment has troubled interpreters unaccustomed to a conjunction between scientific knowledge and esoteric powers, instead of the usual conjunction between science and its technological application. He comments:

> I do not think that Empedocles gave himself over to the practices of a shaman or a miracle worker. His work is intelligible in itself. But, contrary to the tragedians, he says here that nothing, neither life nor death, [which are] mere names, is beyond the reach of the power he possesses.[5]

It is certainly fascinating that Hölderlin sought to write a tragedy about a philosopher whose fundamental views contravene, not only those of philosophers seeking to distance themselves from figures such as prophets or shamans (although even Socrates still resembled the latter in some respects), but also those commonly accepted by the Greek tragedians who subject man to necessity, fate, and death (interestingly, Diogenes Laërtius recounts a narrative tradition ascribing to Empedocles himself the composition of a number of tragedies).[6]

In Fragment 6, Pausanias is enjoined to learn first what are the four "roots" (ῥιζώματα) of all things, to which Empedocles assigns the divine names of Zeus, Hera, Aidoneus (Hades), and Nestis. Wright speculates that the goddess Nestis, otherwise unknown in classical literature (but mentioned also in Fragment 96), may be a Sicilian form of Persephone,[7] in which case the divine names stand in a subtle balance (denoting the two divine couples ruling the visible and invisible worlds), a balance that would not obtain had the elemental root of water been assigned, as one might expect, to Poseidon. The four roots are, of course, also the primordial elements of fire, air, earth, and water, along with their most powerful phenomenal manifestations, among which Empedocles names the sun and flame, the ether, brightness, and sky, the ground or underworld, and the sea or rain.[8]

The four elemental roots are ungenerated and indestructible, so that it makes sense to assimilate them to the governing divinities (who are, in Greek thought, the immortals). On the other hand, even "long-lived gods" are, according to Fragment 23, born out of the interaction of the primordial elements, in contrast to the divine proper, which, according to the *Katharmoi* (Fragments 133 and 134), cannot be brought within the reach of human sense perception. The latter is capable of apprehending things only because the sensory powers are themselves constituted out of the elements (Fragment 103). In Fragment 134, the divine is described (with an echo of Anaxagoras) as "holy mind" (φρὴν ἱερή) which "darts through the whole cosmos with swift thoughts." Wright thinks that even this "holy mind" is composed out of the elements, but that here the elemental roots are held in perfectly balanced proportion.[9] If so, one would need to turn to Empedocles' understanding of proportional relationships and of "holy mind" to get beyond the mere association of the primordial elements with divine names. There is, however, little in the extant fragments that would allow one really to understand the relationship between the sacred aspect and the physical manifestation of the primordial elements.

Hölderlin is interested chiefly in the sacredness of the pure elements as the "genii of the world," and in the new religious perspective that their sacredness opens upon. It appears, from his characterization of Empedocles' spiritual quest in the First and Second Versions, that the pre-Socratic philosopher had initiated him into a way of thinking and articulating philosophically what he had already dimly divined early in life, but as to which the religious and philosophical traditions in which he was educated could offer no guidance. As already mentioned, he puts his character Empedocles into a similar situation and has him seek out the teaching of light itself:

> Oh heavenly light!—Humans
> Did not teach it to me—long already,
> When my longing heart could not
> Find the all-living one, I turned to you.
> Entrusting myself to you like a plant,
> I clung to you blindly in pious delight,
> For it is hard for a mortal to know the pure ones . . .[10]

The Second Version also poignantly stresses the isolation that this quest and its fulfillment have imposed on Empedocles. Since Empedocles the philosopher, however, tended to substantialize or materialize the elemental energies and was not able to develop his understanding of their sacredness much beyond their mere association with divine names, the guidance he could offer to Hölderlin's nascent realization remained limited. This may be one reason why the thematic of the pure elements, of key importance in the First and Second Versions, recedes in the Third Version (it disappears altogether once Hölderlin composes his translations of and commentaries on Sophocles).

For a philosophically far more refined understanding of the primordial elemental energies of earth, water, fire, air, and space (which, in their subtle aspect and sacrality transcend their physical manifestations), he would have had to turn to traditions that, in his historical context, were not accessible to him, such as certain traditions of Buddhist thought (particularly the esoteric traditions).[11]

For Empedocles, the cosmic forces responsible for the combination of the elements—to the point of their in-different fusion in a quasi-Parmenidean *sphairos*, which is presented as the ultimate form of divinity (of which "holy mind" may be a mere remnant)—as well as of their renewed separation and dispersion are Affection or Love (*philotēs*, Aphrodite) and Strife (*neikos*). It is unitive Love that is responsible for the creation of things (it makes little sense to consider Love to be creative only of living beings, as some commentators do, since for Empedocles everything in the cosmos is sentient and thus animate). Friedrich Solmsen takes Strife to be responsible for establishing the structure of the cosmos by separating out the elements into their massed and manifest physical forms, which he, along with some other commentators, takes to be arranged concentrically.[12] Solmsen rightly rejects the postulation of a dual cosmogony, favored by a number of interpreters including J. E. Raven, H. Cherniss, and E. Bignone, according to which both Love and Strife are generative and alternately bring about inverse worlds. Since the focus of the present discussion is not on Empedocles' cosmology and zoogony as such, but on the relationship of his thought to that of Hölderlin, the details of Solmsen's argument will not be examined here (there is no trace in Hölderlin's Empedocles complex of the idea of a dual cosmogony). Suffice it to note that, while Solmsen's discussion of Fragment 17, which is important to the interpretation he contests (since it speaks of "a double genesis of mortal things and a double passing away") is rather brief and focused chiefly on Aristotle's interpretation,[13] the Fragment need not imply a double cosmogony. Love's work of proportional intermixing and of increasing unification culminates eventually in the total or in-different unification of the *sphairos* which, however, is then "shaken throughout" (see Fragment 31) by Strife, making for utter fragmentation and dispersal, which once again allows for the work of Love to begin. Mortal things are then created by the agency of Love in the intermediary periods leading up to the *sphairos* and following again upon its breakup, whereas they are destroyed in the contiguous periods of complete unification and utter dispersal. In the case of plants and animals, of course, there are also specific natural processes of genesis and of destruction in death, which returns the components of living bodies to the elements to be taken up again into new forms of life; one could perhaps similarly describe the formation and disintegration even of land masses or mountain ranges. By the dual genesis and destruction, Empedocles need in fact not have meant more than the twofold way in which such processes can be described, either specifically or in terms of the cosmic cycle or rhythm; but it is more likely that what he was pointing to are the dual roles of Love and Strife in *both* the creation and the destruction of "mortal things." As a post-Parmenidean philosopher, Solmsen notes, Empedocles had to do better than "positing two [ultimate] forms (one of them misconceived)." His, Solmsen writes, "is a philosophically respectable account which safeguards Being," while also safeguarding the phenomenal world.[14]

Empedoclean Love and Strife clearly cannot be discussed apart from outlining the rhythmic pattern of the cosmic cycle. Taking up the question of this cycle again in light of the conflicting claims of Solmsen (as well as of J. Bollack and U. Hölscher), and of the "orthodox" inverse world interpretation (seconded also by W. K. Guthrie and D. O'Brien), A. A. Long asks:

> Did Empedocles advance a theory according to which the constituents of the universe (or reality) alternate between states of total mixture and total separation, with two intervening periods in *each* of which a world like ours comes into being and ceases to be?[15]

His answer, based on careful textual exegesis of relevant fragments, is that the cosmic rhythm is bipolar rather than quadripolar. Love, as already indicated, works to unite all things to the point of perfect fusion, making the emergence of singular things impossible at this point; but Strife then makes its agency felt from within the *sphairos*, shattering what Love had created. The creative work of unification, allowing singular things, including complex organisms, to emerge, can then begin anew. In such a pattern, there can be no world order created solely by Strife. Likewise, however, there can be no world order created by Love alone since its work of unification is dependent upon the separation brought about by Strife and comes up against its limit, reaching stasis, once Strife is maximally in abeyance. Singular things thus owe their genesis to both the disarticulation wrought by Strife and the unification and harmonization worked by Love; and they are destroyed when either of these powers has reached its acme.

Long's analysis departs from Solmsen's by not recognizing separate stages of cosmogenesis and zoogenesis, and by the recognition that the elemental masses (the physically manifest elements) are not already given *ab initio*, to be merely separated out by Strife:

> The clear implication of this text [Fragment 21] is that the sun, air, earth, and water—the main cosmic masses which correspond with the four elements—each consist now [in the world as we experience it] of like elements put *together* by Love . . . Under Strife, there are neither cosmic masses nor living things, since all the elements are ἄνδιχα, divided or apart.[16]

The two extreme yet contiguous points of the cosmic rhythm, the *sphairos* and its dispersal by Strife, are thus limits where cosmic order threatens to disappear or disintegrate; but as soon as either extreme is touched, the rhythm reverses. It is only the dynamic pattern itself that, as Empedocles indicates in Fragment 17 (line 113), is everlasting and unmoving.

Hölderlin was not, of course, interested in cosmic cycles, but rather in a philosophical understanding of history and culture. Rather than seeking to interrelate the one and the many, he speaks, in the Empedocles complex, of the tension between Nature and Art. The editors of the *Collected Works* comment on "Concerning the Tragic" that Hölderlin's tri-phasic analysis of the interrelation between Nature and Art is phrased in terms of "the anthropomorphic guiding concepts of strife (opposition, splitting apart) and reconciliation (harmonic interrelation, unification)."[17] These concepts are really based on Empedocles' cosmic cycle, rather than being anthropomorphic. Hölderlin, however, does not simply echo the Empedoclean notions of Love and Strife in his formulations (nor yet the four "roots" of Empedoclean cosmology in the love and joy experienced by his character Empedocles in his communion with the pure elements). Rather, he rethinks and transforms the Empedoclean unifying and differentiating powers; and the transformation yields the aorgic and organic energies or principles in terms of which he seeks to understand both the relationship of Nature to Art or culture and the historical interrelation of cultures. It is then not an accident that these important concepts first come to prominence in the theoretical texts of the Empedocles complex; for they are not just somewhat arcane poetic notions but spring from Hölderlin's self-immersion in the thought of the pre-Socratic philosopher. Yet the force of his rethinking of these Empedoclean notions needs to be appreciated, for his own two principles are not simply the renamed counterparts of Love and Strife; they are historically, not cosmically, efficacious powers.

The organic principle is the energy of differentiation, articulation, and individuation, responsible for intellectual thought, plastic form, and artistic organization. It is not a power of fragmentation and dispersion, as is Empedoclean Strife, but is, to the contrary, inherently formative. By fixing firm boundaries, it allows singular things to come into their own and become manifest. Hölderlin, true to his understanding of his own Hesperian identity, stresses and honors it by his affirmation of measure and finitude and, more specifically, by his respect for the "firm letter" and the "calculable law" of poetic composition. Its elemental association is with "this earth" which, for the late Hölderlin, is protected by "the more genuine Zeus" who only comes into his own with the ascendancy of Hesperia.

The aorgic energy, though unitive, is fundamentally a power of excess and, in the Sophocles commentaries, of devastation. In "Ground for Empedocles," it is characterized as incomprehensible, un-delimited, and refractory to human feeling.[18] One hears here an echo of the Kantian sublime, but also, as Françoise Dastur suggests, a possible reference to the speculative drive as such, understood as "the desire to escape finitude into death" (she notes that Hölderlin, like Fichte and Schelling, understood Kant as a speculative thinker in the practical domain).[19] The aorgic principle governs Nature which, in the "Remarks on Antigone," is no longer characterized as divinely beautiful or as maternal, but as "ever hostile to man."[20] Fire has a special privilege for Empedocles among the elemental roots, due to its transformative, life-sustaining, and perhaps also solidifying power;[21] and Hölderlin, whose own elemental sensibility is attuned to fire, associates it with the aorgic principle. In the Empedocles complex, fire remains vivifying, beneficent, and beautiful (even though Empedocles dies by self-immolation); but in the context of Hölderlin's interpretation of Sophoclean tragedy, it is the searing "fire from heaven," as well as the element that rules "the wild world of the dead." Fire is also the symbol of the Greek natal gift of "holy pathos," which Greek art had not, as Hölderlin writes to Böhlendorff, attained full mastery of:

> . . . what is properly national [*nationell*] becomes, in the process of educational formation [*Bildung*], always the lesser advantage. For this reason, the

> Greeks are less the masters of holy pathos, because it was natal to them; in contrast they are surpassing in the gift of presentation . . .
>
> I know now that, apart from that which, among the Greeks and ourselves, must be the highest, namely living relationship and destiny, we are certainly not allowed to have anything *in common* with them. . . . But the ownmost must be learned no less diligently than the alien. For this reason the Greeks are indispensable to us.[22]

The unleashed aorgic energy tends to express itself as "eccentric enthusiasm" or as a passion for death (*Todeslust*). If indeed it is "so dangerous," as Hölderlin tells Böhlendorff, "to abstract the rules of art solely from Greek excellence" in a mimetic manner,[23] the danger stems from a failure to pay attention to and cultivate the properly Hesperian gift of "Junonian sobriety." One then finds oneself without the resources to contain the transgressive passion which Hesperian art and culture tend to maximize to the point of surpassing their Greek counterparts due to the energy of Hesperia's own formative drive (*Bildungstrieb*), which seeks to cultivate, and carry to excess, what is alien to it. One can perhaps rank among such transgressive passions the totalizing movements that swept through Europe and devastated populations in the century following Hölderlin's. These events, it needs to be noted, *cannot be spoken of in the language of the tragic*; they shatter the form of tragedy (even though its thought-structure may, as Schürmann argues, offer pertinent insights).

Hölderlin's aorgic principle then is starkly different, in its impact, from Empedoclean "blameless Love," whereas his affirmation of the differential energy of the organic principle is informed, not only by his understanding of the interrelationship between Greece and Hesperia, but also by his concern for tragic structure (here again Bollack's point, mentioned earlier, that the thought of Empedocles is fundamentally not compatible with that of the tragedians may be relevant), as well as by his egalitarian political ideals, in virtue of which he rejects any form of autocratic unification or totalization.

If the doctrine of the elemental roots and antagonistic cosmic forces is fundamental to Empedocles' *On Nature* (leaving out of consideration here his further concern, in this text, with comparative physiology), the *Purifications* sounds a quite different tone. The work is permeated by a consciousness of exile, which resonates throughout Hölderlin's dramatization. The exile from "yellow Akragas" that Empedocles himself seems to have experienced in the later part of his life (see Fragment 112) opens for him unto the exilic character of the mortal condition as such, a condition in which the *daimōn* finds itself incarnated in a "joyless land" ravaged by murder, wrath, disease, and other powers of devastation (Fragment 121). Scholarly interpretation has been concerned with the question of the identity of the *daimōn*, insofar as it seems to retain its self-identity over successive incarnations, and with the further question of whether such identity in transformation is really consistent with Empedocles' cosmology. Charles Kahn, who pursues these questions in an erudite and perceptive analysis, comes to the conclusion that the *daimōn* should be assimilated to the principle of Love itself.[24] Whatever Empedocles' own conception of the *daimōn* may have been, it is not the case that a doctrine of rebirth, or of a succession of interlinked (rather than discontinuous) lives, necessitates the postulation of an entity that transmigrates yet remains self-same. What is clear, at least, is that the Empedoclean *daimōn* is not alien to the primordial elements, since it interacts with them. According to Fragment 115, the fallen *daimōn* has become offensive to the elements, so that, in their material manifestations, they refuse to receive it. Air chases it into the sea, which spews it unto dry land, where it is driven into the solar blaze, only to be hurled once again into the eddies of ether. Presumably it is this very "loathing" on the part of the elements, their refusal to receive the *daimōn*, which precipitates the ensuing diverse births as plant, fish, land animal, or human being (Fragment 117).

The intital transgression that brings about the *daimōn*'s exile and necessitates the long process of purification can be described as a failure of Love, taking the form of bloodshed, slaughter carried out in war, sanctioned or private cruelty, animosity and aggression, as well as animal sacrifice and dietary practices that involve the slaughter and cruel treatment of animals (Fragments 128, 136–141). It is important to note here that impious sacrificial practices, such as a father slaying his child (Fragment 137), as well as destructive vengeance, children killing their parents in the spirit of religious duty, or deluded slayings are the very stuff of Greek tragedy, and of the mythic material it draws upon (one need only recall Agamemnon, Medea, Hekabe, Herakles, Ajax, or Orestes).

For Hölderlin, the thought of the *Katharmoi* not only infuses his tragic paradigm in The Death of Empedocles with the logic of transgression and expiation, it also becomes amalgamated with the Christian logic of redemptive sacrifice. The Hölderlinian Empedocles who freely chooses death, as he does in the Third Version, so as to accomplish the reconciliation of divinities and humans "in accordance with divine law" is no longer akin to the Empedocles of Akragas who understands his own destiny in terms of the purification of the *daimōn* (killing as such, and therefore presumably suicide, counteracts purification). Although Hölderlin, in the Empedocles complex, espouses a tragic logic of sacrifice, he will go on to repudiate this in his translations and transpositions of Sophoclean tragedy, in which, instead, he traces the painful but salutary mutual abandonment of "the god" and man. It is possible, however, that the seeds of this changed understanding were already sown by his reflection on the *Katharmoi*.

FIVE

The Faithless Turning: Hölderlin's Reading of *Oedipus Tyrannos*

> I must underline, however, that only "hyperbologic" is without a doubt equal to giving an account of this schema of "double return" on which Hölderlin's late thought rests, and according to which the very excess of the speculative is exchanged for the very excess of submission to finitude . . .
>
> In sum, tragedy is the catharsis of the speculative.

Given the loss of the manuscripts of Hölderlin's translations of Sophocles' *Oedipus Tyrannos* and *Antigone* and the fact that his epistolary discussion or mention of the translations is limited to six letters, most of them addressed to his publisher Friedrich Wilmans and written between late September 1803 and April 1804,[1] it is not possible to date the inception of the work or to follow its progress chronologically. The translations were published in the spring of 1804 in two volumes, under the general title *Die Trauerspiele des Sophokles* (*The Tragedies of Sophocles*), suggesting a vaster translation project, which Hölderlin was unable to accomplish, though fragments survive.[2] Given his deteriorating mental health, he was also unable to write the general Introduction to "the tragedies" that he had promised Wilmans and had hoped to finish, first in the fall of 1803, then the following spring, or "otherwise at an appropriate time," and finally as a text to be printed separately in the fall of 1804. Therefore, apart from what can be gleaned from the translations themselves, the extraordinarily rich but hermetic "Anmerkungen" ("Remarks," or "Annotations") that he appended to both tragedies,[3] along with two late letters to Böhlendorff,[4] constitute the small but significant textual base from which to glean his late philosophy and poetics of tragedy.

Hölderlin's chief textual source (particularly for *Antigone*) was the so-called *Brubachiana* edition,[5] which was riddled with distortions and corruptions of the Sophoclean texts. These are reflected in the translations and further compounded by mistranslations, as well as by deliberate alterations, on Hölderlin's part.[6] As Jochen Schmidt points out, Hölderlin's concern, as a translator of Greek texts, was not for linguistic accuracy, but for "the essential representations and structures,"[7] that is to say, for the very spirit of the language and the work. Moreover, he sought to make the ancient drama speak a language congenial to a contemporary German audience. Unfortunately, the idiosyncracies of his Sophocles translations, which resulted from these combined factors, made for their uncomprehending and sharply negative critical reception by his contemporaries. Hölderlin's hopes to secure his place among the literary elite with these translations (a place already promised to him by his *Hyperion*), and to have Goethe see to their staging in Weimar, were also bitterly disappointed by the near-betrayal of both Schiller and Schelling, who considered the idiosyncracies of his translations to be evidence of his mental derangement.

A philological study of the translations is a labor which cannot be undertaken here; furthermore, as Bernhard Böschenstein has pointed out, one cannot hope today to present a full synthetic overview of Hölderlin's recreations of Sophoclean tragedy, but only specific analyses.[8] The literality or nonliterality of the translations will therefore be considered here only where relevant to the philosophical thought-structures which are the concern of this book. Given that—their unassuming titles notwithstanding—Hölderlin's difficult "Remarks" on the two tragedies offer the theoretical framework for understanding his translations, while also carrying forward the philosophy of tragedy first articulated in certain of the essays of the Empedocles complex, the "Remarks" will here provide the chief basis for interpretation.

The "Remarks on Oedipus" open with a discussion of the "calculable law" (*das gesetzliche Kalkul*) of poetic composition that, in Hölderlin's view, should form the basis of evaluative judgment, outweighing mere subjective response. This method of creating "what is beautiful" can be learned from the art of classical antiquity, as well as analyzed and perfected by practice, contrary to the prevalent emphasis of eighteenth-century aesthetics on the transgressive role of sheer "genius."[9] Hölderlin, indeed, clung to the "firm letter" even to the point of expressing to Wilmans his preference for the rough, still uncorrected print of his manuscript, on the basis that here, symbolically at least, "the letters that indicate what is firm" maintain their own in the typography and attest to the work's character.[10]

In poetics, the firmness of the calculable law, however, rests, not on substance, but ultimately on vacuity, namely on the "counter-rhythmic interruption" or the sheer empty space of the *caesura*. This is especially true of tragedy, because here the "tragic transport" itself, from which issues the rush of interconnected representations (*Vorstellungen*), is essentially empty and therefore "the least fixated."[11] To present (*darstellen*) itself, tragic transport requires the interrupting *caesura* which, Hölderlin asserts, brings to appear, not the mere sequence of representations, but representation itself, configured over against emptiness.

The *caesura* institutes equilibrium; but this equilibrium is no more mathematically determinable than is the mean that constitutes Aristotelian moral virtue. Hölderlin notes that if the "eccentric rapidity" of the later part of a tragedy's representations pulls along the initial part, the counter-rhythmic interruption must lie close to the beginning so as to protect the latter against the momentum of the pull. Conversely, if the initial sequence of representations is disproportionately weighty and rapid in its rhythm of succession, the *caesura* must lie close to the end, so as to safeguard or strengthen it. In Hölderlin's view, these two inverse compositional models characterize *Oedipus Tyrannos* and *Antigone* respectively; and in each of the two tragedies, the entrance of the blind prophet Teiresias marks the location of the *caesura*. One must then ask oneself what is really brought to pass by the entrance and discourse of Teiresias. Although there is here a parallel between the two tragedies, which Hölderlin evidently perceived but did not address or bring to the fore, the question as to what is the impact of Teiresias's entry upon the tragic stage will, in this chapter, be focused solely on *Oedipus Tyrannos*.

In *Oedipus Tyrannos*, the precipitate rush of representations is initiated by the protagonist's "infinite" or excessively searching interpretation of the Delphic oracle's pronouncement. Kreon's report that Apollo commanded an eradication of pollution (μίασμα; Hölderlin translates as *Schmach*) from the land (OT, 96–98)[12] need, on a more finitizing interpretation, enjoin no more than paying scrupulous attention to the upholding of law and justice and to maintaining good civil order. Teiresias, whom Oedipus has already sent for, would certainly be the authority, not only on how to interpret the oracle, but also on how to root out μίασμα and appease the god. Oedipus, however—the proud "man of experience" whose intelligence has saved the city from the sphinx and who believes, or tries to believe, that he has succeeded in outwitting Apollo's oracle by fleeing Corinth—responds to Kreon's report with a query not only as to the ritual purification supposedly called for (trespassing here on Teiresias's domain of expertise), but also as to the origin of the pollution. Thus, Hölderlin points out, he himself—not the oracle—turns Kreon's thoughts to the unsolved and long-neglected murder of Laios[13] (who had himself, on his fateful journey, been on his way to the Delphic oracle). Kreon's call for the murderer's death or exile (the conventional punishments) thus reflects his own thought process rather than the oracle's injunction. In short order, Oedipus now vows to bring the ancient guilt to light himself, rendering visible what had long remained hidden (and his preoccupation with his own detective work as savior of the city already renders him oblivious to what might truly have been the Delphic message). When the chorus, in the first *stasimon*, beseeches the gods to stem the plague, he tells them to look no further than to his own investigations for the fulfillment of their prayers, and he proceeds to call down a withering curse on the unknown murderer (in one of the play's intricate ironies, he makes a point of not excluding himself from its reach; OT, 253). When Teiresias, impatiently awaited, arrives, his task as a seer has already been narrowly and disastrously circumscribed for him, leaving him no latitude, due to Oedipus's self-blinding rush to conclusions and his consequent rash initiatives: the prophet is called upon to identify the murderer.

Hölderlin himself does not explicitly enter upon the thematic of sight and blindness that is crucial to the tragedy as a whole, and in particular to the interchange between Oedipus and Teiresias. Given that the point of the *caesura* can be and, in this Sophoclean tragedy, demands to be understood as an eclipse of sight or as a blinding that has become irrevocable and leads necessarily to the protagonist's undoing, the analysis of Oedipus's exchange with Teiresias given here will focus on this moment of blinding and on how it is brought about.

Although the blind prophet cannot actually see it for himself (εἰ καὶ μὴ βλέπεις; OT, 302), Oedipus remarks—not without condescension—that he must be keenly aware of the city's affliction and anxious to offer his services within the framework of the king's chosen agenda. When Teiresias makes clear that his own searing vision of the actual state of things does not conform to Oedipus's blindsight, the king rashly accuses him of plotting Laios's murder (which only his visual impairment supposedly prevented him from carrying out in person). Teiresias affirms his reliance on the power of truth; but Oedipus reviles him, rejects his counsel, and mocks his blindness, not dreaming that he will soon be similarly afflicted (OT, 369–373). He is convinced that a seer engulfed by night—and thus ultimately the prophetic vision of Apollo amidst the obscurations of mortal sight—has no power over anyone who can see the plain ordinary light of day in which things stand revealed in their customary identities (OT, 375).

These ordinary perspectives now converge, for him, on the new vanishing point of Kreon's supposed treason (aided and abetted, as he thinks, by Teiresias); and the suspicion, no sooner entertained, passes for compelling fact. He provokes Teiresias at last to tell him the horrific truth to his face; but he has already so blinded himself to it that he can no longer see even what is being held up to his eyes (OT, 412–428). The blank point of the eclipsing *caesura*—Oedipus's retrenchment into a willful self-blinding—is inscribed here. Even though he falters briefly when Teiresias brings up the issue of the identity of his parents, he is no longer capable of self-questioning and thus of gaining fresh insight. The prophet now reveals to him what he himself discerns, at this juncture, not only as to the past and present, but also on the horizon of the future (OT, 447–462). Although once a genuine prophecy has been uttered it cannot be contravened, Oedipus does not confront sheer fate or divine power, but only the full impact of his own willful self-blinding (which, to begin with, is intellectual and spiritual and enacted upon his body only when, at last, he cannot bear to look at what he now is forced to see).

Although Hölderlin, in the middle section of his "Remarks," cites Teiresias's final revelations to Oedipus (OT, 452–460), he does not explicate the *caesura*. What fascinates him in the tragedy is the protagonist's "furious curiosity" (*zornige Neugier*), or the "furious excess" (*zorniges Unmass*) of his spirit, which is torn along by the rush of the time (*die reissende Zeit*).[14] In his second letter to Böhlendorff, he had spoken of encountering, in the south of France, the masculine "wild martial" character, which "feels itself in the feeling of death as though in virtuosity, fulfilling its thirst to know." He reflected that, in experiencing the "athleticism" of southern humanity, he had understood how its members safeguarded their exuberant "genius" against "the power of the element."[15] Oedipus, however, has deprived himself of any such safeguard; and the fury (*Zorn*) that racks his spirit is that of his impassioned self-exposure to the elemental (aorgic) power. Against its searing onslaught, he seeks, until the end, to get a hold on himself and to assert the defining boundaries of his individuality. Here is the source, Hölderlin remarks, of his "foolishly wild" or even "insane" quest for "a consciousness," which leads him, in the end, to cling to straws or to fantasies (such as that of divine parentage), and finally to abase himself to "the rough and naïve language of his servants."[16] He has reached, at the threshold of his undoing, the nadir of his wrath against Teiresias, which he at first voiced pridefully, at a time when, as Hölderlin notes, his quest for knowledge still showed, despite the lack of measure, "its magnificent and harmonious form," seeking heroically to take hold of what it could neither grasp nor bear.[17]

In the brief and hermetic third part of the "Remarks on Oedipus," Hölderlin returns to the question of tragic *Darstellung*. Whereas, in "The Fatherland in Decline," his concern was for the commemorative interiorization and idealization of historical process, through which tragic presentation could achieve meaningful coherence, his stress is now on disjunction and separation. Tragic presentation hinges upon how the monstrous and "limitless" union of the god (the elemental power of Nature, or "rushing time") and of a human being, consummated in fury (*Zorn*), "purifies itself through limitless separation" (which is the true tragic *katharsis*).[18] Through the ensuing separation, what in itself was monstrous becomes capable of self-comprehension, which in turn opens the way for tragic *Darstellung*.

The purifying separation takes on "the all-forgetting form of faithlessness," which is, paradoxically (but with empirical truth), the most memorable. The memory of "the heavenly ones" depends, indeed, on the trauma of this faithless rupture; for, otherwise, Hölderlin writes, "the course of the world" would show a "gap," that is to say, a resistance to comprehension and memory, at the very point of the union between man and divinity (a union that Hölderlin's Empedocles thought he had fleetingly achieved). The *caesura* must be understood as the mark of this purifying separation.

How then does the decisive separation come about? The human being, according to Hölderlin, forgets both itself and the god and "turns like a traitor;" for, at the extreme limit of suffering, man is thrown back on the empty conditions of time and space and on the sheer moment without issue. Thus, he faces the collapse of hegemonic principles or epochal guarantors of meaning. The god, on the other hand, now shows himself under the pure aspect of time, turning "categorically" away from man; for, in sheer time, beginning and end cannot be reconciled, so that history has no intrinsic order, necessity, or *telos*. Man must now likewise become faithless to his guiding initiatives; and so, through devastating loss, the passion for hybristic union or ultimate reconciliation is chastened.

If tragedy, as Schürmann argues, opens upon a vision of original and irreconcilable differing, the catastrophe that reveals tragic truth may symbolically cost the hero his (ordinary) sight, as, Schürmann notes, happened to Oedipus.[19]

Considered as a self-blinding, Oedipus's tragic denial differs nevertheless in some respects from that of Agamemnon in Aeschylus's *Iphigeneia at Aulis*, which is Schürmann's preferred model. Whereas Agamemnon had to veil his gaze (as shown in a Pompeiian fresco that Schürmann mentions), so as not to see his daughter's pitiful supplication and her claim upon his protection, Oedipus blinds himself, inversely and paradoxically, to formless darkness, or to the shadow side of manifestation. It is partly for this reason that Hölderlin describes his tragic transport as empty and without bounds.[20] Rather than fixating on any definable law or principle, Oedipus seeks only the light as such—not indeed the "mild light" that Delia had praised, but a harsh and raking illumination that allows nothing to retreat into the shadows. It is an excess of light that blinds him, both at the point of the *caesura* and when, at last, he cannot bear to see what stands irrecusably revealed.

Oedipus's wife and mother, Jokasta, by contrast, is at ease with the half-light of the mortal condition. Prophetic sight, she tells Oedipus, is worthless. Did it not lead her (when she still accorded it the customary respect) to hand over her own newborn son—his ankles gratuitously pierced and pinned by Laios—to a slave commanded to kill him by exposure? And by heeding the oracle's warning, did she not also, she thinks, effectively invalidate it, at the cost of losing her child? The god, she tells Oedipus, will himself make manifest, with sovereign ease, whatever he deems to be necessary (OT, 724f)—so that, by implication, there is no point to Oedipus's frenzied researches. She tries to soothe his fear of coupling with his mother (a part of the oracle that she and Laios apparently did not themselves receive) by telling him (in strikingly proto-Freudian terms) that there is hardly a man alive who has not done so in his dreams, and that such nocturnal hauntings are best disregarded (OT, 981–984). Her deepest conviction is now that unintelligible chance (τύχη), not lucid necessity, governs the lives of mortals—and of that which chance may bring, no one can have foreknowledge. Rather than trying to dispel the obscurities of the past as well as those of the future, one should, she thinks, concentrate on living here and now as best one can (OT, 977–979).[21]

It is rather astonishing that Hölderlin—who, in his comments on this Sophoclean tragedy, neglects the feminine figure (much as he did in the Third Version of his own Empedocles tragedy)—disregards Jokasta's advocacy of what, in a Nietzschean vein, one could perhaps call a creative forgetting for the sake of life (a forgetting which neverheless will have its costs). This is strange not only because the counterplay between Oedipus and Jokasta, sustained throughout the tragedy, is crucial to its dramatic structure, but also because Jokasta can be considered as one of the Sophoclean counterparts of Hölderlin's own Delia (others being Ismene in *Antigone* and Chrysothemis in *Electra*). There is, however, also a difference between these Sophoclean women and Delia in that the latter refuses neither knowledge nor action; her life-affirmation does not involve, as does Jokasta's, a partial self-blinding to her own past. One wonders, however, if it is ultimately possible to embrace the mortal condition (which is a condition of limitation) without a measure of self-blinding. Jokasta's refusal to know is perhaps the reason why, as David Farrell Krell has pointed out in an insightful discussion of "Sophocles's tragic heroines," Oedipus, in the end, rushes into the palace, not to save, but to kill Jokasta, who has already taken her own life.[22] Her suicide is not the result of her new understanding of her own identity and past, but rather her desperate response to Oedipus's refusal to leave things shrouded (along with his devastating accusation that her only concern, in resisting his researches, was supposedly to safeguard her own noble lineage).

There are, then, two reasons to question Hölderlin's neglect of Jokasta: hers is the voice that, with an echo of Delia's, seeks to restrain Oedipus's "furious excess;" but she is, by the same token, a partner, or the inverse counterpart, in his self-blinding, so that the counterplay between Oedipus and Jokasta becomes, in the end, one between two modalities of self-blinding. The question concerning Hölderlin's neglect of this structure cannot be answered but only raised here, to be kept, as it were, within view at the horizon.

Hölderlin understands Oedipus (and, more problematically, also Antigone) as, in Gerhard Kurz's characterization, "an individuality that posits itself absolutely, or that, what amounts to the same, identifies itself with the god, appropriates the god."[23] Oedipus is, in this respect, for Hölderlin a mythic and tragic character who can symbolize the epochal transition from classical antiquity to modernity, with its shift of focus to subjective consciousness. As such a figure, he stands, like Empedocles, within a turning of the times (*Zeitenwende*); and he is a transgressive individual, necessarily given to excess.

Unlike Empedocles, however, Oedipus does not choose death but becomes a blind exile and wanderer—his destiny is the singularly modern one of exilic itinerancy. Böschenstein points out that the figure of the wandering stranger is, for Hölderlin, that of Rousseau who becomes assimilated to the aged Oedipus in *Oedipus at Colonus*.[24] Oedipus, however, cannot emulate Empedocles (another Hölderlinian figure of exile) in seeking a union with Nature in death, since it is his passion for union (ultimately with the god, but on a more earthly plane also with the woman who bore him) that has led to his doom. It is, parenthetically, striking how Empedocles' leap into Mt. Aetna, spoken of in the Third Version as the "dark mother" opening up her fiery arms, is akin in its symbolism to Oedipus's incestuous union. Even though Oedipus will, at the threshold of death, return, as Böschenstein emphasizes,[25] to the sacred earth and its deities, the stress for him, in *Oedipus Tyrannos*, lies not on union, but on purifying separation.

Irremediable separation is, of course, opposed to the ideal of reconciliation that governs the Empedocles complex. In *Oedipus Tyrannos*, reconciliation is refused as a result of the faithless turning and of the dissociative impact of pain. Tragedy now accomplishes no transformation of the negative into spiritual gain, but rather brings home the epochal disjunctions within historicity as well as the disjunction between end and beginning in individual destiny. When divinity reveals itself as sheer "tearing time" (*die reissende Zeit*), the enthusiasm for an ultimate union with it is shown to be hostile to life and, in fact, to be a passion for death (*Todeslust*).

Hölderlin nevertheless still understands the work of tragedy as salutary and even, in keeping with its ancient ritual origins, as sacralizing. He notes that, when the human being turns away from the god in faithlessness, like a traitor, he or she nonetheless does so "in a sacred manner."[26] *Katharsis*—as Empedocles, the author of *Katharmoi*, well understood—is a sacralizing labor. Lacoue-Labarthe argues that what is purified in Hölderlin's late understanding of tragedy is not only tragedy's speculative appropriation, and perhaps the thought-structure of the speculative as such, but also and importantly a certain religious and ritual logic:

> [Hölderlin's reading of *Oedipus Rex*] is based entirely upon a condemnation, which could not be more explicit, of the indissociably speculative

> and religious temptation, which Hölderlin sees as the basic wellspring of the Oedipean "fable" . . .
>
> [Oedipus's] tragic fault consists then in the religious and sacrificial interpretation of a social ill; and the tragic hero founders, as Schelling would say, due to wanting to accomplish the rite and to desiring a "pharmakos," so as to efface the defilement he imagines to be sacred; he founders, not by directly provoking punishment, but by setting up the old ritual of the scapegoat.[27]

The religious-economic logic that is critically purified here is, in a more refined form, the sacrificial logic of the Empedocles complex, developed most clearly in the Third Version, according to which a singular "chosen One" accomplishes, by his freely embraced sacrificial death, a destinal reconciliation at a critical historical juncture. In a certain sense then, Oedipus, who does not choose death but who stabs out his eyes and becomes a blind wanderer is (not to pun on his feet) the antipode of Hölderlin's Empedocles. Or should one perhaps pay attention to the injured and swollen feet that give him his name? Unlike Empedocles who, in the face of death, feels himself to be buoyant as though capable of flight, Oedipus treads the earth with halting gait; but the earth that he kisses as he is about to die, and that receives him in kindness, is "this earth," the emblem of finitude.

Krell notes Dastur's criticism of Lacoue-Labarthe's thesis that the Hölderlinian *caesura* is the *caesura* of the speculative, which she advances on the ground that, far from interrupting "the speculative process of *Selbstbespiegelung*" or self-reflection, the *caesura* is in fact its condition, as the suspension, in a kind of *epochē*, of "the movement of reality." This critical point, however, is not incompatible with Lacoue-Labarthe's guiding characterization of the *caesura* of the speculative as a "submission to finitude."[28]

Over and above sheer submission to finitude, Hölderlin's late thought is, as already noted, concerned for its sacralization, which displaces the religious logic of sacrifice, and which is accomplished through the turning away from each other of the god and of man in the movement of what Lacoue-Labarthe calls the "double return." Although the sacralization of the finitude of the mortal condition first comes to voice through Delia in the First and Second Versions of *The Death of Empedocles*, Delia is, in retrospect, far too innocent to give it the necessary weight. In this regard she contrasts with Jokasta who, however, cannot sacralize the mortal condition which she embraces since her chief concern is to protect those whom she loves by veiling the truth. The sacralization of finitude requires, for Hölderlin, a passage to "the extreme limit of suffering," which cannot come about in a veiling of sight or in a refusal of memory. At this limit, there remain intact only "the conditions of time or of space," that is to say, a differential spacing or a dissonance that cannot be surpassed by seeking to "rhyme" beginning with end;[29] and this spacing of finitude is what the tragic protagonist at last turns toward and affirms "in a sacred manner."

SIX

Dys-Limitation and the "Patriotic Turning": Sophocles' *Antigone*

Pray I will and sing I must,
And yet I weep—Oedipus' child
Descends into the loveless dust.

If Antigone has retained a power to fascinate and haunt sensibility, thought, and imagination that is probably unrivalled by other tragic characters (only the epic figure of Odysseus seems, in this respect and within ancient Greek literature, her equal), Hölderlin himself indicates the fundamental conditions that empower a poetic work to present such a figure. He opens his "Remarks on Antigone" with the reflection that, whereas philosophy treats only of a single capacity of the soul, so that "the presentation [*Darstellung*] of this one capacity then amounts to the whole, and the mere coherence of the articulations of this same capacity calls itself logic," poetry [*die Poësie*] treats of the *different* capacities of human beings. In poetry, the presentation of these different capacities is what yields a genuine and *differential* whole; and the interrelation of parts then manifests "rhythm" or the "calculable law."[1] As Aristotle points out in the *Poetics*, tragedy is more philosophical than history, which remains bound to the arbitrariness and disconnection of the factual;[2] but for the late Hölderlin, philosophy itself is intrinsically limited, as compared to poetry, due to its predilection for reductive unification.[3]

If Hölderlin, unlike his German Idealist contemporaries, responds to *Antigone*—notwithstanding the tragedy's philosophical near-canonization—

as a poet rather than just as a thinker, a scholarly interpretor who respects his thought and word will herself need to approach the tragedy from out of the full range of her human "capacities": her sensitivity, her gender, her history and life experience, as well as her intellect. Thus, she may sometimes find herself motivated to engage Hölderlin's thought from hermeneutic vantage points that reflect her own historical situation which, at the writing of this book, is that of the first decade of the twenty-first century.

ANTIGONE'S ERRANT "ENTHUSIASM"

Hölderlin characterizes Antigone as a woman whose reason wanders in errancy "beneath the unthinkable;" and he considers that giving voice to such errancy constitutes the ownmost character of Sophocles' poetic language (from a contemporary standpoint, Sophocles would then be, quite surprisingly, a more "modern" tragic poet than Euripides).[4] Since Hölderlin's concern is with how the protagonist is torn away from his or her "midpoint" (a notion already prominent in "Ground for Empedocles") and seized by "the spirit of the ever-living unwritten wilderness and the world of the dead"[5]—and given also that Sophocles has Ismene tell Kreon (who charges her and Antigone with madness) that, at a certain point of outrage, the human spirit falters and gives way (A, 563f)[6]—Hölderlin tends, in his translation, to render the characters' self-expression more extreme by an intensification of Sophoclean diction.

The intensification is particularly striking in his translation of the verses with which he introduces the second part of his tripartite "Remarks," the section that contains his analysis of the tragedy proper. He has Antigone answer Kreon's question as to why she defied his law forbidding Polyneikes' burial as follows:

> Darum, *mein* Zeus berichtete mirs nicht,
> Noch hier im Haus das Recht der Todesgötter . . .
>
> This is why: My Zeus did not announce it to me,
> Nor here in the house the right of the gods of death . . .

The Greek text (at A, 450f) reads:

> οὐ γάρ τί μοι Ζεὺς ἤη ὁ κηρύξας τάδε,
> οὐδ' ἡ ξύναικος τῶν κάτω θεῶν Δίκη . . .

To translate literally:

> It was not at all Zeus who announced this to me,
> Nor yet Dike who dwells with the gods below . . .

Whereas Hölderlin's intensified diction (and otherwise idiosyncratic translation) suggests that Antigone recognizes and follows a god of her own ("*my* Zeus") as well as a law or justice that is linked to the gods of death and that obtains "here in the house," she actually says no more than that neither Zeus (the sovereign Olympian and sky god) nor the chthonic deities have proclaimed Kreon's law to her or affirmed its justice. She goes on to state that divine laws, in contrast to Kreon's edict, are unwritten, unshakeable, and timeless (A, 454).[7]

Hölderlin's reading suggests the interpretation—which can be traced from Hegel (whom he directly influenced)[8] to Schürmann—that *Antigone*, or by extension Greek tragedy as such, is fundamentally concerned with a nomic conflict. For Hegel, moreover (and here again one hears the echo of Hölderlin's *translation* rather than of his thought),[9] the counter-law to the public law, or the law of the state, is, in *Antigone*, the law of the family or the household and its divinities, and thus of woman (whose domain, in ancient Greece, was strictly that of the house, and whose duties included the conduct of funeral rites).[10] If one then reflects on the maximization of certain "hegemonic phantasms" (as Schürmann calls them) in the twentieth century, one suspects that an ethically motivated opposition or resistance to them would have run the risk of being debilitated, from the outset, by an engrained intellectual habit of positing two gender-related nomic spheres, that of the state or of the public domain and that concerned with the private or the singular, and of associating misgivings against the former with unpatriotic, "unmanly," or even "womanish" concerns. Such nomic duality, however, cannot be traced in any straightforward way either in *Antigone* itself or in Hölderlin's interpretation of the tragedy, although, as already pointed out, it is indeed suggested by his *translation*.

In her analysis of Hölderlin's "Remarks on Antigone," Dastur finds there to be a closer link between his thought and translation than indicated here. She recognizes in the "*my* Zeus" of his Antigone her transgressive identification or attempted union with divinity, which takes the form of rebellious insurrection [Hölderlin's *Aufruhr*]:

> [Hölderlin] thus accentuates the opposition between a Zeus who stands surety for an interdiction, and who is the [Zeus] . . . to whom Antigone refers and who, for his part, does not recognize her. It is this personal pronoun "my" that here expresses the dynamics of insurrection. . . . [Antigone] thus also represents an excess of speculative knowledge by which humans pretend to divine vision . . .[11]

In tracing a consummate complementarity, with a view to speculative excess, between Oedipus and his daughter, however, Dastur does not consider Hölderlin's more subtle alterations of the Sophoclean text in the same verses, in that he has Antigone refer to "the gods of death" and locate them "here in the house." It is not evident that these alterations are integral to Antigone's insurrection which, according to Dastur, turns her into a figure of the *antitheos* in the double sense of contending against and seeking to equal divinity.[12]

In the tragedy, the chorus of conservative Theban elders notes indeed that the uncompromising extremity of Antigone's passion resembles her father's (A, 471f); yet Antigone, quite unlike Oedipus, remains acutely mindful of the limits set to mortals. Whereas Oedipus strives relentlessly to bring all things to light—even those he cannot bear to see—Antigone's passion is rather for leaving darkness intact. This darkness, however, is not the protective half-light that Jokasta cultivates, nor is it akin to Ismene's averting her gaze from the dead and their lot while affirming her bond to the living. Ismene reproaches Antigone that she has "a warm heart for the cold," that is, for the dead (A, 88); but it is Antigone who takes to heart the chorus's admonition in the first *stasimon* that death alone (Ἅιδα μόνον, that is, Hades as *A-idēs*, the Unseen) sets an absolute limit to human ingenuity and mastery (A, 361). This is the darkness she respects and wants to leave inviolate.

Antigone is mindful of the likelihood that not only explicit, humanly instituted laws, but the very distinctions between friend and enemy, patriot or traitor, that, in ancient thought, were basic to law as well as to ethical life, are not recognized in the sightless realm of the dead (A, 519, 521). Impiety does not lie, for her, in violating any particular body of laws (such as the laws pertaining to the family or the house, nor yet those concerned with the performance of sacred rites), *but in daring to extend humanly instituted law beyond the limits set by death to human understanding and power*. In the name of the infrangible darkness of Hades, or of the enigma that surrounds mortal life, she resists the self-exaltation of Kreon, "the new man for a new day" (A, 156f), and the proponent of autocratic rule. What she fundamentally resists, in the name of the enigma of which death is the placeholder, is the transgressive maximization of hegemonic principles, and thus absolutization and totalization.

This analysis is, to be sure, not entirely congruent with Hölderlin's reading of *Antigone*. He hears her crucial question to Kreon, asking who on this earth can really claim to know that "those below" would not find Polyneikes' burial pure and uncorrupt (A, 521f)—to which Kreon quite predictably replies that an enemy remains an enemy alive or dead—as attesting to her gentle reasonableness in misfortune. He also finds it characterized by a dreamy *naïveté*, rather than appreciating the forcefulness of her refusal to assimilate the sightless realm of the dead to the panorama of human sight. He does, however, hear in her question the most proper tone of Sophocles' poetic diction.[13]

Despite its gentle tone, Antigone's reflection that, in the sightless realm to which all must pass, the antithetical articulations that define life in the *polis* lose their binding force is crucial in that it marks her passage into "dys-limitation" (*Entgrenzung*). In an event of dys-limitation (this neologism will be retained here), the epochal constraints that govern and enable a certain modality of historical human existence are eroded so that an individual drawn into this event is drawn into an empty infinitude. Hölderlin understands Antigone to be seized, in this sense, by an "infinite enthusiasm" that negates the measures of finitude; and it is the force of this dys-limitation that sets her adrift "under the unthinkable." If, as Dastur points out, she loses, like Oedipus, any sense of the distance separating humans from divinity, she does so, not willfully, but because the measures of finitude fail her. Whereas Oedipus labored under an excess of interpretation or of a will to blinding clarity, Antigone faces a darkness impenetrable to human sight. On Dastur's reading, the divine laws that she relies on lack only universality and the force of command:

> [T]hey can never be thought abstractly, but [can] only present themselves in a particular case and action. These divine laws, as to which Hölderlin underscores that they are unwritten in the sense of not being prescribed, are immanent in the act which manifests them . . . Antigone, by her act, . . . pretends to know the divine in an immediate and private manner.[14]

Perhaps, nonetheless, Hölderlin's understanding of the "unlettered wilderness" into which "the tearing spirit of [the] time" (*der reissende Zeitgeist*) pulls Antigone is more desolated still than is indicated by the laws' lack of universality and commanding force. If so—and this issue remains still to be explored—Antigone may find herself in the end unable to recognize any law inherent or manifest in her own action and destiny.

What precipitates the draw into dys-limitation need not be a world-shaking event. The exposure of Polyneikes' corpse to the elements and the devourers of carrion is, to be sure, an abomination; yet is not Antigone's forfeiture of her life for one already dead itself, as Ismene thinks, an excessive response? Hölderlin addresses this question:

> The boldest moment of the course of a day, or of a work of art, is reached where the spirit of time or nature, the heavenly that seizes man, and the object that interests him, are most wildly opposed, because the sensory object reaches only halfway; *but spirit awakens most powerfully where the second half begins*. At this moment, man *must hold fast the most*; for this reason, he also stands here most revealed in his character.[15]

One would fail to grasp the momentum of the dys-limiting event in seeking to economize occasion and response according to a logic of loss and gain (whether in the mundane or the Idealist sense). The actual occasion only provides the breach for the incursion of the dys-limiting force. Antigone, drawn into epochal discordance, must "follow the categorical [turning of] time categorically," that is, without reserve.[16] The epochal turning that Hölderlin has in mind is the specific transition from the Greek to the Hesperian configuration, which will need to be traced out here, since it is crucial to his understanding of the tragedy, and of tragedy as such.

THE GREEK/HESPERIAN CHIASM

Although Hölderlin had long been preoccupied with the differential relationship between classical antiquity and modernity, or "Oriental" Greece and Hesperia, this question took on a new urgency for him at about the time of his journey to and return from Bordeaux in 1802. At the same time, his image of classical Greece darkened, compared to the image reflected in his epistolary novel *Hyperion*, veering from the idealization and nostalgia common among German intellectuals of the time to a recognition of the excessive, transgressive, or, as Dodds was to call it, "irrational" momentum at the heart of the culture.[17] In his letter to Böhlendorff of 4 December 1801 (commenting on the latter's "dramatic idyll," or modern tragedy, *Fernando*), Hölderlin argues that the vivid clarity and lively plasticism of presentation characteristic of the Greek genius cannot be surpassed—but *not* because these sprung from its incomparable natal endowment. Rather, Greek thinkers and poets were driven to learn and pursue lucidity of presentation by the artifice of cultural formation or *Bildung* so as to attain the "*free* use" of their own genuine yet dangerous natal gift: the passionate intensity and "holy pathos" that Hölderlin calls the "fire from heaven."[18] He now experiences this elemental power (akin to the aorgic principle) as threatening with a devastating *ekpyrosis*, and with drawing those who are receptive to it into "the fiery world of the dead." Thus, in the "Remarks on Oedipus," he characterizes the figure of Teiresias (in both the tragedies he translated) as standing "guard over the power of Nature which tragically transports man out of his sphere of life . . . and tears him into the eccentric sphere of the dead."[19]

For the Greeks, their counter-natural accomplishment of consummate lucidity and plastic articulation, together with what Hölderlin, in his second letter to Böhlendorff (undated, but written after his return from France), refers to as the "athleticism" of southern cultures, and as the Greek heroic body, enabled them to protect their native genius against "the power of the element," and against its own tendency to destructive excess.[20] In contrast, the Hesperian natal gift of clarity and restraint threatens, on its negative side, with a dearth of passion, grandeur, or a sense of destiny. As Hölderlin tells his friend, what among Hesperians counts as tragic is that: "[w]e take leave from the land of the living very quietly, enclosed in some sort of container, not that we, consumed by flames, atone for the flame that we were unable to subdue."[21]

Nevertheless, he adds, if a tragedy is artfully written, the perdition of its hero will evoke terror and pity and focus thought on Jupiter's glory, whether it follows "our own or ancient destiny."

The traits natural to the Greek genius are what the Hesperian formative drive tends toward and what needs to be cultivated so as to allow the Hesperian natal gifts to attain their full artistic expression and flourishing; for, as Hölderlin points out, the ownmost must be learned no less than the alien, and "the *free* use of *one's own* is what is most difficult."[22] As Dastur notes, Greek art and culture is not, for Hesperia, a model which could be statically imitated, but rather an example to be creatively heeded:

> We can draw a lesson from the loss of the Greeks in this sense: that what caused their ruin, the obsession with form . . . can incite us to turn our [own] cultural tendency, [oriented] toward the unlimited, in the opposite direction, and to orient it toward our terrestrial nature.[23]

Oedipus Tyrannos can be understood as a tragedy of the maximization of the Greek formative drive (*Bildungstrieb*), expressed here as a relentless passion for lucid self-understanding (in this sense, Oedipus is a proto-Hesperian figure). Since Oedipus becomes alienated from his natal affinity to the fiery element and thus finds himself incapable of a free relationship to his destiny and of the sovereign use of his proper gifts, the "flame" destroys him. Parenthetically, when Hölderlin writes to Böhlendorff in the second letter that "the powerful element, the fire of heaven . . . has constantly gripped me, and . . . I probably can say that Apollo has struck me,"[24] one can interpret his own affliction as attesting to the excessive pull exercized on him, as a Hesperian poet, by the Hesperian formative drive, which seeks out the Greek-Oriental fire.

If Antigone is, in contrast, and as Dastur notes, a profoundly Greek tragic heroine, the reason is that she wholly relinquishes herself to the Greek elemental "fire." In *Antigone*, Hölderlin, who considers himself quite free to alter "the holy names under which the highest is felt," regards only one thing as strictly unalterable: "how in the midst time turns . . . how a character follows the categorical time categorically, and how one passes from the Greek to the Hesperian."[25] These moments of turning and of passage must not be conflated; and both must be explored.

One sense of the "midst" as the location of time's turning is the interrelation between Antigone and Kreon. Hölderlin takes pains to point out that this interrelation is quite other than that between Ajax and Odysseus (in Sophocles' *Ajax*), which interconnects the "national" with the "anti-national," which is "the formed" or the cultivated [*Gebildetes*], and is likewise other than that between the Greek "original nature" and the pursuit of the Greek formative drive. Antigone and Kreon stand, he finds, in a dynamic equilibrium and "differ only according to time," so that the "gain" or the more powerful impact lies with the new initiative, which is Antigone's.[26]

The "gain" she achieves is what Hölderlin calls "the patriotic turning" (*die vaterländische Umkehr*), which is not a turning toward, but a revolution *within* the *patria*, here the Greek configuration. This is why Hölderlin can comment that Sophocles insightfully presented "the destiny of his time and the form of the fatherland."[27] In *Antigone*, the turning comes to pass in the manner of a rebellion (*Aufruhr*), which is reactive, so that "what is without form is inflamed by the overly formalized."[28] What the revolt reacts against is a condition of rigidity or sclerosis that has resulted from the excesses of the Greek formative drive and that has not only restrained but even denied and suppressed the Greek natal endowment. As concerns Kreon (of whom Hölderlin gives, in the interest of showing the dynamic equilibrium, an overly serene characterization), the excess and sclerosis take the form of an empty self-absolutization of sovereignty as a kind of self-willing will. As Haimon charges pointedly (at A, 739), his father would do well ruling over a desert all by himself.

Although the patriotic turning challenges and subverts sclerotic excess, its initiation is not a benign event since it involves "the turning around of all the ways and forms of representation," so that "the entire aspect of things is changed."[29] In other words, it involves a passage through dys-limitation. To acknowledge this, however, is also to acknowledge that dys-limitation can happen *within* the parameters of a given epochal configuration, which raises the question as to what then is the relevance of such an event to the epochal transition from Greece to Hesperia.

Given the inverse relationship between their respective natal endowments and formative drives, Greece (with its Oriental provenance) and Hesperia are, for Hölderlin, chiasmatically linked by an interconnection that forms the figure of infinity (∞).[30] This interconnection is the fundamental reason why the epochal disjunction between Greece and Hesperia preoccupies him to the exclusion of other epochal disjunctions, such as those due to conquest and colonization, that he might otherwise have reflected on. An event of dys-limitation *within* the Greek configuration is especially danger-fraught because it destroys the protective lucidity and measure that Greece had cultivated, unleashing the full wildness of the fiery, aorgic element. Since the Hesperian formative drive tends toward this very fire and sense of destiny, the Greek dys-limitation constitutes for Hesperia a warning example which holds it back from following the sheer onrush of its own formative drive. One can reflect here on what it may have meant—beyond Hölderlin's historical horizon—for twentieth-century Germany to maximize the tendency of its cultural formative drive in a quest for grandeur and a sense of destiny, while neglecting the free and creative (rather than obsessive or servile) cultvation of its natal tendency to lucid ordering. It remains, of course, a consummate historical irony that Hölderlin's thought and art were themselves (without benefit of attentive explication) annexed and exploited by the Third Reich.[31]

In the "Remarks on Antigone," Hölderlin compares the Zeus of the ancient world, who "*merely pauses* between this world and the wild world of the dead," to the "more genuine" or "more proper" (*dem eigentlicheren*) Zeus watching over Hesperia, who "*forces* the course of Nature, ever hostile to man . . . *more decisively toward this earth*."[32] This second Zeus safeguards the

Hesperian gift of "Junonian sobriety;" and here one must recall the association of Zeus's spouse Hera (Juno) with the earth element. As Beda Allemann (taking up the contrast between model and example) sums up:

> [For Hölderlin,] the *decline* of the model furnished by the Greeks . . . is integrated into an argumentation that aims at founding a new exemplarity of Greek artistic practice. This stroke of genius . . . permits Hölderlin to draw in a single trait of the pen the consequences of the fatal unilateralism of Greek artistic practice and . . . to safeguard their [the Greeks'] exemplarity for Modernity. The Greeks . . . help us as concerns the mission of becoming inhabitants of this Earth; and the emblem of this mission rightly bears the Roman name of the Greek spouse of Zeus: Junonian sobriety.[33]

Given Hölderlin's democratic and egalitarian ideals, however, he is not content to leave the transition to a Hesperian ideal of "inhabiting this earth" merely at the level of an abstract or mythic discussion. As in the final testament of Empedocles in the First Version, he offers at least a glimpse of its sociopolitical implications. He notes that the "form of reason" (*Vernunftform*) that takes shape amidst the wildness and terror of a tragic time acquires, in a "more humane time," the aspect of a firm and divinely sanctioned conviction; and, in such a time, the tragically engendered new form of reason "is political, namely republican." Within *Antigone*, Hölderlin points to the equilibrium maintained between Kreon's passion for rulership and Antigone's resistance, as well as to the circumstance that, in the end, Kreon, in a subversion of sovereignty, is "almost brutalized by his servants."[34] The epochal disjunction between Greece and Hesperia can, he thinks, point the way, for moderns attentive to its tragic dynamics, to a salutary transformation of ethical and political life.

THE BLINDING *CAESURA*

In *Antigone*, the counter-rhythmic interruption or *caesura* marked by the late entrance of Teiresias also indicates the culminating intensification of an accelerating rhythm of efforts at persuasion. Although it differs, in this respect, from the *caesura* in *Oedipus Tyrannos*, Kreon's encounter with Teiresias, like that of Oedipus, also leads up to the eclipsing *punctum caecum*, the point at which the protagonist's tragic blindness becomes total and irreversible. Hölderlin's comments on the *caesura* in *Antigone* concern only its positioning within the "rhythm of representations." An effort to show its eclipsing dynamics will therefore not explicate, but rather supplement, Hölderlin's analysis.

Although Kreon's edict denying burial to Polyneikes is repellent to the chorus from the outset,[35] they voice a strong warning, which constitutes a somewhat veiled attempt at persuasion, only in the second *stasimon*, when

Kreon has already condemned Antigone to death. What the chorus warns of is the ἄτη sent by the gods to a human being misled by hybristic desire. Given that ἄτη means not only calamity or ruin, but also delusional folly or blindness (Hölderlin translates the term as *Wahn* and *Wahnsinn*, "delusion" and "madness"), the warning is consummately phrased: one who allows himself to follow "much-wandering hope" and misguided passion will not notice the delusion creeping up on him so that, to someone whom the gods lead swiftly and inexorably to ἄτη, evil will appear as good (A, 615–625).

Haimon, who enters while the chorus is still speaking, makes the effort at persuasion explicit and intensifies it, moving from the skillful establishment of a common basis (by granting Kreon's presuppositions) to increasing and, in the end, utter frustration and anger at his father's egomania, retrenchment in injustice, misogyny, and gratuitous cruelty. At the conclusion of his "Remarks on Oedipus," Hölderlin therefore points to Haimon in *Antigone* as a character who parallels Oedipus, in that he "must follow the categorical turning, so that in what follows he cannot equal the initial" (that is, he cannot remain true to his earlier self).[36] Haimon, the dutiful and well-spoken son who ends up despising his father, and who kills himself with the sword with which he had lunged at him and missed (A, 1233–1235), ranks, for Hölderlin, with Oedipus in exemplifying man's tragic "unfaithfulness" at the point where he is "wholly in the moment."

Teiresias arrives unbidden when every attempt at persuasion relying solely on human wisdom has already failed. Like Haimon, Teiresias seeks to persuade (καὶ σὺ τῷ μάντει πιθοῦ; A, 992) by first establishing a shared basis—here he reminds the king of his own esteem for the seer's long and valuable service to the *polis*—but his advice springs purely from his gift of prophetic sight. He directly challenges Kreon's deepening moral and spiritual blindness by the straightforward revelation that Kreon's own deluded heart-mind (φρήν) is what is setting an imminent plague upon the city (A, 1015). This revelation, however, only provokes Kreon's derision and far-fetched accusations. Citing the commonly accepted ancient religious view that no mortal can possibly afflict the gods with μίασμα, he reasons with twisted logic that he is therefore free to defile their altars and sanctuaries with bird-borne carrion in the most outrageous way (A, 1039–1044). Teiresias, who had initially warned Kreon that he was standing precariously on the razor's edge of fate—a position of *krisis*, but not as yet of doom—at last finds himself provoked, now that the king's tragic denial has become irrevocable, to prophesy his doom. Although, once a genuine prophecy has been uttered, no fear-inspired change of heart can alter the imminent course of events, these follow strictly from the protagonist's own actions. Teiresias further reveals to Kreon that he has offended the sight of both the heavenly and the chthonic divinities by immuring a living being in a rock-hewn tomb, while exposing a corpse, belonging to the netherworld, to the stark light of day. These willful offenses against the sight of the gods will—even though mortals cannot afflict them with μίασμα—provoke them to punish him who commits them with blinding ἄτη. The exposure of a corpse is particularly heinous in the case of Polyneikes, Kreon's kinsman; but it is further compounded by the exposure of anonymous enemy corpses left to rot on the battlefield. Teiresias points out to Kreon that the tide of outraged anger and grief that normally follows war (but without being trained on any one particular person) now rises up against him and is about to engulf him (A, 1185–1205). Although the *caesura* lies at the point of the eclipse of sight, this eclipse is not lasting (and maybe the Erinyes see to that). When sight (in the metaphoric sense) reawakens, directly revealing to the protagonist his offenses and delusions for what they are, it becomes an inescapable torment.

ANTIGONE'S DESOLATION

As Antigone is about to be led to her live entombment, the chorus, maintaining the "cold neutrality" that Hölderlin finds "peculiarly appropriate," tells her that, in going alive to Hades (as well as in other respects), she follows a law of her own (she is αὐτόνομος; A, 822).[37] Antigone's self-comparison, in response, to the Phrygian Niobe, legendary Theban queen who, in her grief, was changed into a rock formation on Mt. Sipylus, is of special importance to Hölderlin. His translation here departs extensively from the Greek, in particular in introducing the figure of the desert. Hölderlin has Antigone say:

> Ich habe gehört, der Wüste gleich sei worden
> Die Lebensreiche, Phrygische.
>
> I have heard that, like unto a desert, became
> She, rich in life, the Phrygian.[38]

The figure of the desert, though incongruous with that of the ice-melt that, as "snow-bright tears," constantly washes over the rock formation, is tellingly appropriate to Antigone herself, the gatherer of dry dust with which symbolically to bury her brother's corpse, and a betrothed young woman denied marriage and childbearing. In her self-comparison to desolated Niobe, Hölderlin hears a tone of "exalted scorn" and "holy madness" that, to him, conveys the highest reaches of the human spirit as well as "heroic virutosity" and supreme beauty.[39]

In its secret travails and in highest consciousness, he reflects, the soul may paradoxically seek to evade consciousness by comparing itself to a lifeless thing that yet symbolizes a form of consciousness, or it may counter the spirit or the god who is about to seize it with derisive or even blasphemous speech, which nonetheless safeguards "the holy, living possibility of spirit."[40] It does so to shatter the outworn and ossified forms of spiritual life, allowing it to effract new pathways.

Niobe, the figure of hybristically exuberant fertility rendered childless and desolate, is, for Hölderlin, the very "image of early genius," as well as of the destiny of "innocent Nature." There is, for him, no original desert; rather, the land, responding with hightened fertility to the solar radiance in a kind of aorgic rapture, is driven toward the "overly organic," and thus toward barrenness. Antigone's fate seems less than analogous, since she strives desperately but vainly for the organicism of self-consciousness, or for a delimited individuality and a culturally recognized self-image, as she is about to be seized by the god "become present in the form of death."[41]

Although the chorus cruelly rejects her self-comparison to Niobe on the grounds that she is a mere mortal, whereas Niobe was of divine birth, it takes up her quest for a mythic narrative and identification that would render her fate comprehensible, but only in the fourth *stasimon*, when she has already been led away to her death. The three mythic figures invoked—Danaë of Argos, Lycurgus of Thrace, and Cleopatra, daughter of Boreas and Oreithyia[42]—have no link to Thebes and share with Antigone and each other only harsh imprisonment and subjection to the power of fate. Hölderlin's comments focus exclusively on Danaë who, after Zeus visited her in the form of light, carried his "golden-streaming seed" in her womb (A, 950). In a deliberate alteration of the text, which he justifies as bringing the thought closer to contemporary modalities of representation, he translates:

> She counts for the father of time
> The hours struck, the golden ones.[43]

Zeus, Hölderlin writes, should, in serious speech, be called "father of time," or "father of the earth," since "it is his character, contrary to the eternal tendency, to turn around *the striving out of this world into another, to a striving out of another world into this one*."[44] Zeus is not only the divine figure who sets in motion the patriotic turning, he is also the one whose "rays of light" render time calculable. Danaë counts the golden hours for Zeus because when, as Sophocles says, she had to leave the heavenly light for the darkness of the brazen vault that imprisoned her (A, 943f), she could no longer look ahead to any future. Whereas reason extrapolates from the present to the future, time, according to Hölderlin, becomes truly and simply "calculable" only in suffering, but not calculable in an economic sense or in the manner of historical understanding and projection. Rather, human sensibility, in deprivation and pain, is aware only of the simple passage of hours or of the empty form of time. Hölderlin's discussion here parallels his statement, in the "Remarks on Oedipus," that in the extremity of suffering, there obtain only the empty conditions of time and space.[45] In tragic extremity, then, a dialectical philosophy of history, an eschatology, or a doctrine of the incursion of the divine into history, such as Manes puts forward in *The Death of Empedocles*, must collapse, along with any theory of tragedy that seeks to transmute loss into spiritual gain. Time marks the empty measures of finitude, so that a god who is "nothing but time" must necessarily turn away from man in unfaithfulness. However, Hölderlin notes, a "firm abiding before the changing time" constitutes a heroic and hermitic mode of life and is as such "highest consciousness."[46] It is this sober consciousness, achieved in the extremity of pain, that firmly resists the death-bound pull of "eccentric enthusiasm." Here then it is no longer a marginalized voice, such as Delia's, that recalls the tragic characters to their finitude. This recall is now the cathartic work of tragedy itself, symbolically presided over by Zeus, the "father of time."

It is true, to be sure, that the poignancy of the Sophoclean Antigone does not fully come to word in this analysis. Although she has enacted, out of her respect for the darkness or enigma that mortals face in their dying and that negates the absolutization of any principle or instituted law, a courageous deed of love (*philia*) and of reverence, she has done so without either divine or secular sanction. She has no validation and no home, she fears, either with the living or with the dead; and her last plea, as she is led to her entombment "unwept, unloved, and unwed," is only for the elders and the men of the city to grant her the simple recognition of their look. It is questionable whether human sensibility can really endure being thrown back upon the empty passage of time; and it is telling that Antigone, unlike Oedipus and Kreon who live out their lives and go on to interpret their destinies, will strangle herself as soon as the burial chamber is sealed.

Nicole Loraux points out that Sophocles does not speak of her death as being αὐτόχειρ ("by her own hand"), as he does speak of Haimon's and Eurydike's suicides (but not of Jokasta's). To her own question of whether Antigone's death, on which action "has left no trace whatever" so that one hears only of her inert body, escapes by its retrenchment into passivity and silence "the discourse of the auto-affection of the same," she answers in the affirmative. Not only does nothing belong to Antigone less than "this death that she is not even said to have given herself," but also, in her annihilation, "the impossible identity of a *genos*" that has exhausted itself in its quest for self-reflection is undone.[47] Although Hölderlin's analysis does not do full justice to Antigone's desolation, it does capture the subversion of reflection that Loraux indicates.

TRAGIC PRESENTATION AND THE FAILURE OF *MIMĒSIS*

Returning, in the third part of "Remarks on Antigone," to the question of tragic *Darstellung*, Hölderlin considers that, in tragedy, "infinite enthusiasm," or the rush to immediate union with the god, must be purified by separation, so that oppositional forms of consciousness confront and sublate one another and the god at last becomes present in the form of death.

This is brought about in fundamentally different ways in the Greek and Hesperian tragic modalities. In the former, the tragic "word" (which is "more interconnection than pronounced, [and] in a destinal manner moves from beginning to end") is mediately efficacious (*faktisch*) in that its force seizes the actual human body, driving it to kill. In contrast to this "dangerous form," which Hölderlin terms "deathly efficacious" (*tödlichfaktisch*), a Hesperian mode of (re)presentation allows the word to seize instead "the more spiritual body" so that (in a manner prefigured by *Oedipus at Colonus*) "the word out of an inspired mouth is terrible and kills" without the physical body's being driven to murder or suicide. Although Hölderlin calls the Hesperian tragic word "deadly efficacious" (*tötendfaktisch*), he notes that, in the Hesperian context, tragedy need not issue into murder or death. The difference between the two tragic modalities can be traced to the fact that, given the Greek natal gift of passionate enthusiasm, the challenge here is "to get a hold on oneself," (which brings with it an emphasis on physicality, plastic form, and "athleticism"), whereas, in Hesperian representation, the challenge is "to have a destiny."[48]

What changes the force of the tragic word in the Hesperian context is that "we stand under the more genuine Zeus" who not only "pauses between this world and the wild world of the dead" (thus stemming the rush of passionate enthusiasm), but who also forces "the course of Nature, ever hostile to man" decisively toward the earth.[49] The Greek poetic forms and modalities of representation, Hölderlin says firmly, need to be subordinated "to those of our native land" (*dem vaterländischen*), so that the "deathly efficacious" tragic word must also recede in favor of the word that directly seizes "the more spiritual body." If one looks back from this perspective to *The Death of Empedocles*, one sees that this tragedy could not, for Hölderlin, ultimately succeed, since it remains caught up in a mimetic relationship to Greek forms of thought and artistic (re)presentation, particularly in that the tragic word here remains "deathly efficacious" in its unswerving focus on Empedocles' sacrificial death. In contrast, the Sophocles translations involve an effort meaningfully to transmute Greek poetic forms, bringing them close to their Hesperian counterparts. Hölderlin's very translations thus abandon the mimetic mode.

Lacoue-Labarthe adds a further insight to Hölderlin's break with a mimetic relationship to classical Greece. Greek art (understood in a wider sense, as encompassing intellectual creation), is, he points out, all that still remains of a mode of being "irreversibly fled, lost, forgotten." However, precisely because it is *art* (and thus the creation of the Greek formative impulse or *Bildungstrieb* rather than a straightforward expression of the Greek natal character), it cannot possibly put one in touch with what was genuinely Greek. Lacoue-Labarthe puts this point even more radically: "*What is proper to the Greeks is inimitable because it has never taken place*;" and he concludes:

> Greece will have been, for Hölderlin, this inimitable. Not by an excess of grandeur—but by a failure of the proper. Greece will thus have been this vertigo and this menace: a people, a culture, indicating, and not ceasing to indicate, themselves as inaccessible to themselves. The tragic as such, if it is true that the tragic begins with the ruin of the imitable, is the disappearance of models.[50]

If, furthermore, the disappearance of models is intrinsic to dys-limitation, it bespeaks itself most trenchantly in Hölderlin's reflections on *Antigone*.

Even though the Greek and Hesperian tragic modalities diverge, the poetics of tragic presentation requires, in each case, a forceful dialogical interchange and choral commentary. Hölderlin had introduced a chorus only in the Third Version of his Empedocles tragedy and had left the first and only choral ode a short fragment. Nonetheless, he considers dialogue and choral parts to be "the *suffering organs* of the divinely striving body," which are indispensable since divinity must be "intellectually grasped or appropriated in a living manner."[51]

Whether Greek or Hesperian, no effort to grasp the infinite, "such as the spirit of states and of the world," can proceed otherwise than from a partial and skewed perspective (*aus linkischem Gesichtspunkt*). Native (*vaterländische*) poetic forms are preferable where available, not because they bring one any closer to an absolute standpoint, but because philosophical understanding alone is not, as it were, the whole story. The native forms "do not serve to enable one just to grasp the spirit of the time, but to hold it fast and to feel it, once it has been comprehended and learned."[52]

Insofar as a natal (or patriotic) turning is at work in *Antigone*, and given that such a turning changes the entire aspect of things, it is essential, Hölderlin writes, that each of the *dramatis personae* should, "as seized by an infinite reversal, and deeply shaken by it, feel itself in the infinite form in which it is [thus] shaken."[53] Hölderlin's emphasis on feeling as the indispensable complement of intellectual thought would seem to have a certain relationship to the return to earth mandated by the "more genuine Zeus," given feeling's openness to the singular in its finitude. Art then would not exhaust itself in the sensuous presentation of the idea; but *aisthēsis*, which brings together feeling and sensuousness, would remain insurpassable. Hölderlin, however, does not comment on the place of feeling within the turning; and this place could not be defined in terms of the Greek/Hesperian chiasm that he delineates. The fact that, as Dastur points out, feeling (or *aisthēsis*), for Hölderlin, always passes through or relates itself to "something higher . . . that must be honored"[54] constitutes indeed a common bond between him and the Greek poets most significant to him: Homer, Pindar, and Sophocles.

SEVEN

From an Agonistic of Powers to a Homecoming: Heidegger, Hölderlin, and Sophocles

. . . Denn vieles vermag
Und die Flut und den Fels und Feuersgewalt auch
Bezwinget mit Kunst der Mensch
. . . aber er steht
Vor Göttlichem der Starke niedergeschlagen . . .

. . . For much he is capable of,
And flood and rock and the power of fire
Man vanquishes by art
. . . but he stands
Beaten down, the strong one, before what is divine . . .

Greek tragedy is, for Heidegger, an initial and significant modality of thinking the being of beings in its essential interrelation with and differentiation from becoming (*phainesthiai*) and semblance (*Schein*), as well as thinking (*Denken*) and obligation (*Sollen*). In *Introduction to Metaphysics* of 1935, Heidegger understands *Oedipus Tyrannos* as "a single strife between semblance (concealment and dissemblance) and unconcealment (being)."[1] Oedipus's driving passion is for the uncovering of being (*Seinsenthüllung*), and if he thus has, in the Hölderlinian phrase, "perhaps an eye too many," this excessive eye is, Heidegger reflects, "the fundamental condition of all great questioning and knowing."[2]

In the context of questioning the interrelation of being and thinking with a view to the essential character of *logos*, Heidegger moves from a discussion of the "poetic thinking" (*das dichterische Denken*, that is, a thinking that is genuinely philosophical rather than technically scientific) of Parmenides and Heraclitus to the thoughtful poetic articulation (*das denkerische Dichten*) of Greek tragedy. He focuses on Parmenides' statement that τὸ γὰρ αὐτὸ ἔστιν νοεῖν τε καὶ εἶναι ("for both are the same, to think and to be")[3] characterizing νοεῖν not as thinking in the modern sense, but as a receptive apprehension or *Vernehmen* of *apophainesthai* or presencing. Since an understanding of νοεῖν, in this sense, is needed to determine the essentiality as well as the historicality of the human being "out of the essential belonging together of being and apprehension [*Vernehmung*]," while nevertheless the path to such an understanding is obstructed by much of the history of Western thought, Heidegger addresses a poetic text that speaks of the essentiality of the human being in a complementary way: the first *stasimon* of *Antigone*. To undo the obstructions to genuine understanding that prevail even here, he reflects that a certain license of translation and interpretation may prove necessary; and he acknowledges that he cannot, in this context, do full justice to scholarly issues. He also acknowledges that his analysis will not be able to base itself on the tragedy as a whole, let alone on the Sophoclean corpus. With these qualifications, he undertakes an interpretation of the choral ode that follows out three trajectories: seeking firstly what is crucially at issue in the ode as a whole and inspires its linguistic articulation, exploring secondly the dimension opened up by its strophic order or sequence, and lastly taking the measure of human being as characterized by the poetic word.

THE FIRST TRAJECTORY OF INTERPRETATION

The first trajectory follows out, as the guiding insight of the Sophoclean ode, the essential trait of human being in virtue of which man is spoken of as τὸ δεινότατον, the most awesome among πολλὰ τὰ δεινὰ, the multitude of awesome things encountered.

The word δεινόν, which Heidegger prefers to translate, not as "awesome," but as "uncanny" or "un-homelike" (*das Unheimliche, das Unheimische*, in the sense of that which dislocates one from all comfortable familiarity), carries, as he points out, two meanings. Firstly, it indicates what overwhelmingly prevails or holds sway (*das überwältigende Walten*), which characterizes all that is as a whole, in its very being. What makes it uncanny is that it continually expropriates one from any accepted framework of interpretation, and thus from all that one may cling to as habitual, assured, or "non-endangered"—from the lighted precinct, as it were, within which humans seek to define themselves and to map out their lives. Yet humans are in no way alien to το δεινόν in this first sense. On the contrary, they are essentially and therefore relentlessly exposed to it and drawn into it in that they bring to pass being's self-disclosure. Since such disclosure involves bringing all presencing into some configuration of un-concealment, it is necessarily forceful or even violative, so that man is δεινόν also in the second sense of the term: he actively exercizes power (*ist gewalt-tätig*) within the overpowering. This exercise of power is violative in that it disturbs or unsettles any pregiven interpretation, thus once again transporting humans into "the unhomelike." The human being is δεινότατον because these two aspects, exposure to the over-powering and the power of a disclosive response to it, converge in human essentiality.

If, as Heidegger holds, the insight that man is surpassingly uncanny and essentially without home offers "the genuine *Greek* definition of man," it is important to consider how this exilic condition comes about. This requires, Heidegger points out, an appreciation of "the power of semblance [*Schein*] and of the struggle [*Kampf*] with it as it pertains to *Dasein*'s essentiality."[4] He will enter fully upon this question only in the following trajectory; but here he develops, in a preparatory manner, the point that it is man's very resourcefulness that ultimately leaves him without resource. He highlights Sophocles' artful juxtaposition παντοπόρος ἄπορος ("all-resourceful; without resource") in verse 360 of the second strophe of the first *stasimon*; glossing over the fact that these terms end and begin statements, respectively, and are therefore, in modern editions, separated by a semicolon.[5] Whereas the Sophoclean statement that all-resourceful man ἄπορος ἐπ' οὐδὲν ἔρχεται / τὸ μέλλον translates straightforwardly as "without resource he never meets up with what lies ahead," Heidegger's translation (which encompasses also the adjective παντοπόρος) is both artful and surprising:

> Überall hinausfahrend unterwegs, erfahrungslos ohne Ausweg, kommt er zum Nichts.
>
> On his way voyaging out along every course, inexperienced, without recourse, he arrives at nothingness.[6]

As one who, on every ingenious course, finds himself without recourse, man, Heidegger indicates, is deprived of any relation to a possible home (*dem Heimischen*) and is exposed to ἄτη as perdition or disaster.

With a parallel focus on Sophocles' second antithetical phrasing ὑψίπολις ἄπολις ("exalted within the city; deprived of city") in verse 370 of the second antistrophe (and with a similar disregard for the fact that these adjectives, usually separated by a semicolon, respectively end and initiate different sentences), Heidegger indicates that the *polis* constitutes the ground or place where the eventful and resourceful courses followed out by *Dasein* intercross, so that the *polis* emerges as the site of history (*Geschichtsstätte*). He understands the *polis* here as a nucleus of human creative agency, arguing that its poets, thinkers, priests, and rulers are what they are only insofar as they exercise violative power (*Gewalt*). As creators, they are not bound by limits, laws, and structures; for it is up to them alone to initiate these for the *polis*.[7] This leaves them deprived of city or site, solitary, uncanny, and without recourse among beings as a whole.

THE SECOND AND THIRD TRAJECTORIES OF INTERPRETATION

The second trajectory, which follows the strophic sequence, starts out from a consideration of man's relationship to the elements (Sophocles names sea, storm or air, and earth, of which Heidegger conflates the first two). In sharp contrast to the reverent and inspired intimacy of Hölderlin's Empedocles with the primordial elements, the relationships outlined here are violative and geared to mastery. Heidegger characterizes man's relationship to sea and earth as a setting out (*Aufbruch*) and incursion (*Einbruch*), respectively (as does not appear in English, both terms are variants of "breaking" or "breaching"). Nevertheless, he stresses that these efforts at mastery serve to reveal that which overridingly prevails as inexhaustible donation (*spendende Unerschöpflichkeit*), sounding here at least an echo of the sacrality and generosity of the Hölderlinian elements, or perhaps rather of what Hölderlin calls Nature.

The first antistrophe takes up the theme of mastery by characterizing man's relationship to animal life as what Heidegger terms "capture" (*Einfang*) and "subjugation" (*Niederzwang*). Since Sophocles' explicit mention of fish, birds, and land animals correlates with his three elements, the sense of human mastery over these primordial powers is re-enforced.

As concerns the human powers foregrounded in the second strophe: speech, thought, emotion, law, political organization, and medicine (Heidegger omits the latter but stresses passion), Heidegger argues that they do not constitute human attainments but rather penetrate human being to its core, instead of merely surrounding it. Thus, these powers, which characterize the human being, introduce alterity or uncanniness into his or her very self.

The human being's violative effraction of pathways to his goals leaves him or her, Heidegger stresses, ultimately with no way out (*auswegslos*). Why? Not because of any failure of ingenuity, but because their very ingenuity entangles humans in semblance (*Schein*), so that, as they turn in every conceivable direction (in *Vielwendigkeit*), they find themselves debarred from an opening unto being. Moreover, and crucially, every ingenious pathway is also obstructed and despoiled by death. Heidegger emphasizes that human beings come up against death, not just when dying lies immediately ahead, but constantly, because essentially.

One must agree with Heidegger that here the Sophoclean projection of the power of mortals in relation to being inscribes its own limits; but one must also ask whether these limits are the only ones to be marked. In the first *stasimon*, such is the case; but in the full sequence of choral odes, other limits are inscribed: Eros and Aphrodite, "never conquered," in the third *stasimon*, the curse and ancestral sorrows of "the house" in the second, sheer cruel fate (rather than intelligible divine justice) in the fourth, and finally Dionysian *mania* in the fifth and last *stasimon*. Heidegger ignores this further exploration of human disempowerment. What interests him instead is *technē*, insofar as it plays into the interrelation between human power and what overpoweringly prevails, and thus into man's emergence as το δεινότατον. Here (still within the second trajectory) he follows out three further avenues of thought. The first of these considers *technē* as "the entire range of machinations [*Machenschaft*, the Sophoclean μηχανόεν] consigned to [man]." However, *technē* is not, in Heidegger's understanding, a doing or making, but rather a knowing that enables one to set being into the determinacy of a work. The form of *technē* that outstandingly accomplishes this is art:

> [Art] brings being, that is, the appearing that stands within itself, most immediately to a stand within something that presences (a work). The work of art is not a work first of all because it is worked, that is, made, but because it brings into work [*er-wirkt*] being within a being.[8]

In its very appearing (*Erscheinen*), the art work renders being, thought as *physis*, or as an arising into presences, compellingly manifest in its radiance (*Schein*). Here then the violative power exercised by man, or *technē* understood as τὸ δεινόν, brings to pass a disclosure of being within beings and counteracts entanglement in semblance (*Schein* in its negative sense).

Secondly, whereas the Sophoclean chorus, wary of human arrogance from the outset, emphasizes the constraints of divine and earthly justice, Heidegger thinks δίκη or justice as the alter-aspect of τὸ δεινόν and thus as that which both resists and encompasses human initiative. He calls τὸ δεινόν in this sense by the names of jointure, fitting-together, or disposition (*Fug*, *Fuge*, *fügen*, and their variants). Any merely moral or juridical understanding of *dikē* or justice, he argues, will deprive the notion of "its fundamental metaphysical content." Furthermore, to fit together or to conjoin is also to gather into an articulation, so that *physis* as "originary gatheredness" is both *logos* and *dikē*.[9] In *Dasein*'s essential historicity, *technē* and *dikē* strive against each other.

In the third consideration, Heidegger returns to the thought of τὸ δεινότατον as the interrelation of the two aspects of τὸ δεινόν, that is, of *technē* and *dikē*. Man, possessed of the knowing that constitutes *technē*, effracts the jointure and pulls or draws (*reisst*; like "to draw" the German verb has two senses, though its kinetic sense is more violent) being into a configuration of beings without thereby mastering it.[10] Human being is then tossed about, in danger and homelessness, between jointure and dis-jointure (*Un-fug*):

> He who wields violative power, the creator who marches out into the unsaid, who breaks into the unthought, who forces what has not happened to

> come about, and who makes appear what has not been seen, this wielder of power stands at all times at risk. . . . The more towering the summit of historical *Dasein*, the more yawning the abyss for the sudden plunge into the unhistorical . . .[11]

This consideration leads on directly to the third trajectory of interpretation which, Heidegger admits, is itself necessarily violative, namely of the text, since it must show what is said without its having actually come to word, that is, it must penetrate into what Heidegger likes to call the essential unsaid. If the interrelation of human power and being's over-power opens unto the possibility of a loss of recourse or abode, or unto disaster, this is not, he argues, due to any mere mishap that one could guard against. Rather, disaster or perdition (*der Verderb*) is integral to τὸ δεινότατον in that a violative exercise of power against being's over-power must be shattered if being is to prevail as *physis* or as the arising that holds sway (*das aufgehende Walten*). Human being, furthermore, must necessarily exercise violative power, courting perdition, so that being's over-power may reveal itself:

> *Dasein* means for historical human being: to be set up as the breach which the over-power of being breaks open in appearing, so that this breach may itself be broken apart by being.[12]

With heroic-tragic pathos, Heidegger argues that the violative creator therefore has no regard for goodness, solace, approval, or validation, since perdition is, for him, "the deepest and most far-reaching yes to what over-poweringly holds sway;" for it is only "*as history*" that what thus prevails, being, "confirms itself through a work."[13]

THE DISTANCE FROM HÖLDERLIN OF HEIDEGGER'S FIRST READING OF *ANTIGONE*

In *Introduction to Metaphysics*, Heidegger briefly discusses Hölderlin as being, together with Hegel, under the spell of Heraclitus, but with the difference that "Hegel looks backward and concludes, [whereas] Hölderlin looks forward and opens up." He adds that Nietzsche's understanding of Greek thought is—despite his espousal of the traditional opposition between Parmenides and Heraclitus—exceeded in profundity only by Hölderlin.[14]

Despite his praise of Hölderlin's reading of Greek thought, however, Heidegger does not engage with Hölderlin's philosophy of tragedy in his own discussion of *Antigone* in this text. The resonances of his discussion are Nietzschean, with echoes also of Schelling's understanding of tragedy, and with a fundamental concern for power in its differential relationships.

In his analysis of the will to power as art in his Nietzsche lectures of 1936–1940, Heidegger characterizes Nietzsche's Dionysian art impulse as an antidote to a Wagnerian "conception and appreciation [of art] from out of the mere condition of feeling itself. . . ."[15] This Wagnerian conception could perhaps, in Hölderlinian terms, be regarded as an aberration of the Hesperian formative drive. In the context of a trenchant critique of Wagner's ideal of the *Gesamtkunstwerk* ("total work of art"), Heidegger comments: "The intensification into surges of feeling had to provide the missing expanse for a grounded and fitting [*gefügte*] position in the midst of beings, such as only great poetry or thinking can offer."[16]

If Wagner sought a sheer intensification of and a self-abandonment to "transport arising from intoxication," which might be considered an affirmation or "saving" of life in an increasingly destitute time, Nietzsche, Heidegger reflects, endeavored to bring genuine Dionysian energy into delimited and compelling forms. There seems to be an opening here for thinking this in-forming and delimiting of Dionysian energy in relation to Hölderlin's resistance to "tragic transport" or "eccentric enthusiasm;" but Heidegger does not make this connection. Rather, in *Introduction to Metaphysics*, he thinks the espousal of finitude and historicality in terms of the violative autonomy and essential solitude of the creator who accepts the despoilment of every work. The tone of heroic-tragic pathos sounded by his discussion is a tone not heard in Hölderlin's return to finitude and to a temporality without issue.

The Schellingian echo is well summed up by Jean-François Courtine's remark that Schelling (in the *Letters on Dogmatism and Criticism* of 1795–96) sees in tragedy, and in particular in *Oedipus Tyrannos*, "the heroic figure of an equilibrium between the power or 'superior strength' (*Übermacht*) of the objective world and the self-affirmation of the I in its absolute freedom (*Selbstmacht*)."[17] Heidegger, who understands the underlying conflict as one between *technē* and *dikē*, does not, however, follow Schelling's exaltation of tragedy (in his *Lectures on the Philosophy of Art* of 1802–03) as, to quote Courtine once more, "the absolutization of freedom in its identity [or in-difference] with necessity."[18] Tragedy is not, for Heidegger, a dialectical work of bringing about this in-difference, but rather the revelation, through the necessary shattering of human initiative and power, of being's over-power (which cannot, for him, be assimilated to the objective world or to necessity). Here again Heidegger affirms an agonistic of powers, such that being can only reveal its own over-power in its devastating response to a challenging provocation by human power. It is therefore the heroic and tragic figure of man itself which is "most uncanny" and without an abode among beings, rather than humans' being, in all aspects of their existence, drawn into being's uncanniness—a draw that will more fully inform Heidegger's 1942 reading of *Antigone* in the context of his lecture course on one of Hölderlin's great stream-hymns.

HEIDEGGER'S SECOND READING OF *ANTIGONE*

Heidegger returns to the issue of tragedy in the early and mid-1940s, in his remarks on Hölderlin's Empedocles fragments of 1944 and in "The Saying of Anaximander" of 1946, but above all in his 1942 lecture course on Hölderlin's hymn *Der Ister*, which opens with a citation of Antigone's injunction to the men of her *polis* to look at her, as a bride for whom no nuptial hymn will be sung (verses 809, 814).[19]

That a major part of this lecture course is devoted to *Antigone* is not the result of digression; for Heidegger holds that Hölderlin maintained a constant conversation or interlocution (*eine ständige Zwiesprache*) with its first *stasimon*, not only at the time of the composition of his major hymns, but even during the long years of his illness.[20] This sustained dialogue with Sophocles, moreover, is not a Hölderlinian idiosyncrasy but is called for or necessitated in that "Hölderlin's concern is for the coming-to-be-at-home of historical man," which must pass through an engagement with what is alien yet essentially akin:

> The resonance of the first *stasimon* of the Sophoclean tragedy *Antigone* in Hölderlin's hymnic poetry is a historical-poetic necessity within the history in which the being at home and being homeless [*das Heimisch-und Unheimischsein*] of occidental humanity is decided.[21]

Pointing to τὸ δεινόν as the essential word not only of the *stasimon*, but also of the tragedy, and even of ancient Greek existence (*des Griechentums*) as such, Heidegger offers an interpretive translation that brings out its intercalated yet oppositional meanings and connotations. Firstly, τὸ δεινόν is the fearsome (*das Fürcherliche*) in the two senses of what frightens or terrifies (*das Furchtbare*) and of what commands respect and so is worthy of honor (*das Ehrwürdige*). Either sense implies the perceived possession of power, which itself can take two forms: the exalted (*das Überragende*) is akin to what deserves honor, whereas the violative (*das Gewalttätige*) draws close to the fearsome. In both these further senses, moreover, τὸ δεινόν is also the unaccustomed (*das Ungewöhnliche*), as which it may be either the uncannily excessive (*das Ungeheure*) or that which asserts itself *within* what is customary by a stupendous universal facility (*das in allem Geschickte*). Such facility (*Allgeschicklichkeit*), Heidegger remarks, approaches the fearsome and violative by an "inflexibility of levelling" which allows nothing to escape.

In its essence, τὸ δεινόν, however, cannot be parcelled out into the triplicity (redoubled in each case) of the fearsome, the powerful, or the extraordianry, nor is it somehow the amalgam of these different determinations. Heidegger chooses to indicate the unitary essential sense of τὸ δεινόν as *das Unheimliche*, which will here be translated somewhat awkwardly (so as not to confuse it with *das Ungeheure*) as "the unhomelike" (which tends as such also to be uncanny). While he acknowledges that this interpretive translation does not have lexical sanction, he affirms its deeper insight and characterizes the very term, τὸ δεινόν, as itself *unheimlich* or possessed of uncanniness.

Although man is, in a privileged and genuine sense, δεινόν, so that being unhomelike and uncanny is the fundamental human way of being, uncanniness as such (*die Unheimlichkeit*) does not originate in human existence. Rather, Heidegger stresses, human being (*das Menschentum*) comes out of homeless uncanniness and abides in it. He takes such abiding to be what is indicated by the verb πέλειν in the first verse of the *stasimon* (noting that Hölderlin translates this verb "in an entirely pale and indeterminate manner" as "is" and "there is").[22] Since the human being is essentially without home amidst the configurations of beings, he or she cannot come to rest:

> . . . sea and land and wilderness are the domains which man creatively transforms with all his ingeniousness [*Geschicklichkeit*], using them and making them his own, so that he may find what is there for him [*sein Hiesiges*]. The homelike is sought and striven for by a violative passage through what is unaccustomed for sea and earth, and thereby it is precisely not attained.[23]

Humans are "possessed" by, and therefore obsessed with, what might offer a home or abode to them. In all their resourceful engagement with and fixation on beings (which is, in a hidden way, motivated by this obsession), they grasp, in the end, only "nothingness" (because being, or the very presencing of what presences, is non-entitative). It is for this reason that their all-resourcefulness constantly leaves them "without resource," and conversely, this deprivation spawns an all-resourceful or universal facility which yet cannot attain what it seeks.

Heidegger points out that the tragic negativity that comes to word here has been lost sight of, due to "the Platonic-Christian degradation of negativity," and further that the inability of "metaphysics" genuinely to think the negative is not remedied by the effort of German Idealism (he names Hegel and Schelling) to transmute it into positivity and redeem it. He still finds a "reflection" of this attitude toward negativity in Nietzsche.[24] Insofar as Hölderlin is not, in Heidegger's view, caught up within the thought-structure of metaphysics, he would therefore emerge as a thinker capable of doing justice to the tragic.

In Heidegger's second reading of *Antigone*, then, humans are exposed to, and are bearers of, the homeless uncanniness of being, not insofar as they are violative creators confronting the shattering of work and self, but rather in virtue of a draw that obscurely yet irrecusably permeates human existence. It is this draw, felt as a lack, that motivates and always despoils all resourceful endeavors, given that it cannot be satisfied by any positivity.

Heidegger's concern with a lack which the interpretation of tragic negativity has failed to do justice to is tied up with the affirmation of a "having" that is inalienable: man, in the Aristotelian phrase, is ξώον λόγον ἔχον, the living being who has speech—or, in a formulation Heidegger prefers, it is language that has man. Man is ξώον πολιτικόν, the animal who lives "politically," only in virtue of being ξώον λόγον ἔχον. For Heidegger, however, this does not mean that humans are fundamentally "political" because they converse with one another, that is, because *logos* forms a dialogical bond between them. *Logos* does not, for him, essentially interlink humans; rather, humans are called to address beings in speech (*ansprechen*) with regard to their being. What humans essentially are can then not be determined "politically" (Heidegger comments sarcastically on the claim that the ancient Greeks, in understanding "everything" politically, were "pure National Socialists"—not, however, without adding ambiguously that National Socialism has no need of scholarly validation).[25] Rather than being explicable as a type of state, then, the *polis* is the "stead" (*Stätte*) of human historical abiding in the midst of beings. As such it demands and remains worthy of questioning.

Heidegger questions the *polis* both in this lecture course and in his subsequent lecture course on Parmenides.[26] In both texts, he emphasizes that the *polis* must be understood in terms of the verb πέλω (or πέλομαι) as it figures in the opening verse of the first *stasimon* of *Antigone*, and which is to be heard as an ancient word for being. The *polis* is then πόλος, the pole around which all presencing turns.[27] Its "polarity" concerns beings as a whole, or "beings as to that around which they . . . turn."[28] Humans relate themselves essentially to this pole; and in this sense the polis is "the place-ness [*Ortschaft*] for the historical abiding of Greek humanity."[29] It is notable that Heidegger's dismissal of the explicitly political character of the *polis* as nonessential is tied up with his silence concerning the political aspects of Hölderlin's thought.

The "polarity" of the *polis* means that, as the "stead" of human abiding in the disclosedness of beings, it is complicit in the contrariety that renders the human being surpassingly uncanny (δεινότατος). Heidegger (who notes that Nietzsche treasured a transcript of Jacob Burckhardt's 1872 lecture course concerning the sinister aspects of the *polis*)[30] comments:

> [I]t is of the essence of the *polis* to precipitate into excess and to tear into a plunge, so that man is sent and fitted into both these contrary modalities. . . . Homeless uncanniness (*die Unheimlichkeit*) does not just follow from this dual possibility; rather, the homelessly uncanny (*das Unheimliche*) itself is that wherein the concealed and question-worthy ground of the unity of the duality holds sway, from which the latter has what makes it powerful [and] what carries man up high into the uncanny and tears him along into the practice of violence [*Gewalttätigkeit*].[31]

Continuing with his interpretation of the *stasimon*, Heidegger characterizes the daring (τόλμα) which issues into what "what is ignoble" (τὸ μὴ καλόν) as a relinquishing of the beings revealed within the open span of presencing to a forgetful endangerment of presencing itself (in the mindfulness of which alone humans could find their home). Although his discussion somewhat disconcertingly does not address the concrete nature or political basis of violence, he does caution throughout against a simplistic understanding of these, remarking pointedly that, whereas the *polis* was unconditionally worthy of questioning (*das Fragwürdige schlechthin*), the political in the modern sense counts as what is just as unconditionally beyond question.[32] With a focus on the concluding verses of the *stasimon* (v. 371f), in which the chorus banishes the perpetrator of hybristic daring from the hearth, Heidegger poses the question whether Antigone, who is after all a human being prone like others to such daring, is included within the scope of this rejection and banishment.

This question leads him on to a painstaking examination of the tragedy's opening interchange between Antigone and Ismene. Unlike most commentators, who are inclined to dismiss Ismene (and similarly Chrysothemis in Sophocles' *Electra*) as cowardly, compliant, preoccupied with expediency, or at best uninteresting, Heidegger understands her to articulate a crucial counterposition to Antigone's, so that their dialogue resembles "the encounter of two swords," and the challenge is "to apprehend something of the lightning flash that shines forth from their hitting one another."[33] Nonetheless, his focus remains trained entirely on Antigone; he does not seek to hear in the hesitancy voiced by Ismene a countertone to (self)sacrificial enthusiasm, or to what Hölderlin calls a passion for death—a tone first sounded by Hölderlin's own Delia.

Antigone is, for Heidegger, a woman who takes as the guiding and initiatory principle (ἄρχη) of her action that against which nothing can avail (ταμήχανα, verses 90 and 92), because it is what destinally comes to appearance (*das Zu-geschickte-Erscheinen*; ἐφάνη).[34] As the first *stasimon* states, what disempowers all human initiatives is "death alone" (v. 361). To Ismene, Antigone's resolve to honor an obligation toward the dead at the cost of her own life is to engage in a futile "hunt" (θηρᾶν, recalling, as Heidegger notes, the reference to hunting in the *stasimon*'s first antistrophe) within the realm of human disempowerment. However, Antigone does not seek inappropriate mastery. Rather, she declares herself willing to take upon herself and "to suffer this disempowering uncanniness" (παθεῖν τὸ δεινὸν τοῦτο; v. 96) as the very principle of her mortal being. Her openness to her mortality, however, does not translate into a self-destructive courting of death. Heidegger remarks here that what provides the measure of the tragic in the Greek context is "the truth of being on the whole, and the simplicity with which it comes to appearance."[35]

Antigone thus shows herself, for Heidegger, to be homelessly uncanny in the highest and unconditional sense; but, he asks, does she not perhaps, in letting herself be permeated to the core by this exilic condition, safeguard "the most intimate belonging to the homelike?"[36] The home which she safeguards is not the *polis*, but rather the "hearth" of all presencing (ἑστία, as heard in παρέστιος, v. 371), with its illuminating and purifying flame (fire or flame has for Heidegger none of the negative connotations it has for the late Hölderlin). This hearth is the very being of beings or *physis* as "the self-arising radiance that is not mediated by anything but is itself the midst."[37] Antigone's homelessness amidst the configurations of presencing gathered around the pole of the *polis* then reveals itself to be, not the hybristic excess of those whom the chorus condemns and rejects, but rather the "being homeless in coming-to-be-at-home" which marks the human being's responsive belonging to being itself.[38] When the chorus banishes anyone given to hybristic daring from the hearth, it seeks, according to Heidegger, to come to terms with the contrariety inherent in τὸ δεινόν, and to set apart a homelessness that ensues from seeking one's abode within being from the homelessness of a self-dissipation among beings. The chorus's banishment therefore does not, he reflects, strike Antigone. Nonetheless, the home she seeks within being, and thus within homeless uncanniness itself (in a certain alienation from beings), may appear as sheer nothingness in the face of death and of the refusal of mythic, religious, and kindred or social sanctions. Although Heidegger briefly and in a somewhat veiled way acknowledges this,[39] his analysis does not do justice to Antigone's desolation.

THE CHIASM LINKING HEIDEGGER AND HÖLDERLIN

Unlike Heidegger's discussion of tragedy in *Introduction to Metaphysics*, his second sustained engagement with tragedy (specifically with *Antigone*) takes inspiration from Hölderlin. Indeed, Heidegger not only comments on Hölderlin's tragic thought (with reference to the "Remarks," the Empedocles corpus, and the letters to Böhlendorff), but he also examines details of Hölderlin's translation of *Antigone*. One needs then to ask how the transformations in Heidegger's thought on the tragic may reflect his intensive dialogue with Hölderlin.

Heidegger's fundamental concern in the lecture course on *Der Ister* is for "the coming to be at home of the Germans' historical modality of human existence [*des . . . Menschentums*] within occidental history;" and he considers Hölderlin to be the first thinker who "poetically experiences the German crisis [*Not*] of being without home," and who also articulates the law that governs coming-to-be-at-home.[40] He understands the bond between Hölderlin and Sophocles (specifically as to the much-discussed choral ode) to be their "same" concern, in difference, for the coming-to-be-at-home of German and Greek humanity, respectively. Given this sameness without identity, Heidegger espouses Hölderlin's rejection of a mimetic relationship (*Angleichung*) between Germany and Greece. However, he seems not to be attuned to Hölderlin's warning as to the potential for destructive excess inherent within a culture's unchecked formative drive. Thus, he comments with sanguine enthusiasm that the Germans, in learning the free use of their natal gift (the Hesperian gift has, for him, become restricted to the German), may yet "surpass the ownmost of the Greeks in what is alien to them (the 'fire from heaven')" so as to institute an abode for the gods "with which the temples of the Greeks can no longer compete."[41]

It will not be possible here adequately to examine Heidegger's overarching concern with historicity and German destiny, let alone to enter into the crypto-political dimensions of his thought, or specifically of his engagement with Hölderlin in the historical context of the National Socialist distorting appropriation of the poet's thought (to point out this still unexamined connection is not, of course, to suggest any straightforward complicity on Heidegger's part). The scope of this concluding discussion must therefore remain restricted to tragedy and the tragic.

Most conspicuously, Heidegger's second reading (which is gentler in tone and more probing) abandons his earlier focus on man as a violative and solitary creator and on the historicizing dynamics of the creation and shattering of works. The figures of the priest, ruler, thinker, and poet (all implicitly male)[42] are displaced by Antigone herself as a figure of sheer exposure; and violative power has been relegated to the dangerous side of one of the contrary articulations of τὸ δεινόν. Given that homeless uncanniness in no way originates with humans, the agonistic of powers has ceded to the quest for a homecoming to the unhomelike, which is being's emptiness (even though, in the overall structure of the lecture course, one must question the relation of Antigone's tragic homecoming to the occidental or German homecoming that Heidegger envisages on the historical horizon). Similarly, the contrariety of *technē* and *dikē* no longer has a guiding interpretive role; it belongs, perhaps, among the "polarities" that deploy themselves around the pole of the *polis*. The homecoming that Antigone seeks transcends not only the *polis*, but also the ouranian and chthonic deities—the very dimensions of the cosmos—without this transcendence reaching any positivity. For this reason, it is Antigone's very mortality and honoring of the dead (rather than any works) that allow for a transcendence in which negativity is in no way transmuted or sublated (yet does not approach nihilism).

The marks of Heidegger's engagement with Hölderlin can be traced in his turn from an agonistic of powers to the significance of disempowerment, and from the perdition of the creator and the shattering of works to mortality as not only the trait of finitude, but as enabling a homecoming to homeless uncanniness. There are, however, also aspects of Hölderlin's thought on tragedy that Heidegger bypasses. Most strikingly, perhaps, he disregards the political and ethical aspects of Hölderlin's reading of *Antigone* as a drama of insurrection (*Aufruhr*). These aspects are indissociable from the "natal turning" as Hölderlin delineates it. It will be helpful here to recall his actual words:

> . . . [I]n natal turning, where the entire form of things is changed, nature and necessity, which always remain, incline to a new form . . . [so that even] one who is neutral, and not only one who is moved *against* the natal form, may

> be forced, by a spiritual power of the time, to be patriotic [and] present, in infinite form, the religious, political, and moral [form] of the fatherland . . .
>
> The form of reason which tragically takes shape here is political, namely republican . . .[43]

Despite her disempowerment, Hölderlin's (and Sophocles') Antigone is not ineffectual within the *polis*; she transforms its order.

On a deeper level, one might also question whether the finitizing force of Hölderlin's tragic turning as the mutual abandonment of divinity and man (explored in the "Remarks on Oedipus") has an echo in Heidegger's reading. Not only does Heidegger's Antigone remain entirely true to herself (as perhaps she would not, if he truly thought her desolation);[44] but, in that she attains a coming to be at home in the unhomelike, divinity does not reveal itself to her as sheer time, marked by the empty counting of hours. She is not, in other words, thrown back unto sheer finitude, but initiated into a deeper truth. Her passion, for Heidegger, is akin to the aorgic passion for the "fire from heaven," which motivates the Hesperian formative drive (whose dangers he seems not to recognize), rather than to the embracing of "this earth" enjoined by the Hesperian Zeus.

These reflections are, of course, not intended critically since, as Heidegger emphasizes, one certainly cannot expect two essential thinkers who think "the same" to be thinking the identical. They are intended, rather, to begin to trace the chiasm that both interlinks and sets apart Hölderlin, as a thinker on tragedy, and his most searching twentieth-century interpreter and partner in dialogue, Heidegger. As Heidegger himself would probably put it, this chiasm remains worthy of questioning.

Epilogue

> Who says law (*das Gesetz*) says posit (*das Gesetzte*), and who says posit says halt and the halted, thetic act and tragic denial. A knowledge that should keep us from being startled when (the lesson of the tragedians) the good reveals itself in double prescriptions.

Hegel situates tragedy not only within ethicality, but also within the domain of law as the scene of nomic conflict or, in Schürmann's terms, of double prescriptions, and of the quest for a justice that brings these imperatives into balance.[1] Hölderlin situates tragedy in the context of an epochal transition that exacerbates the conflict between the aorgic and the organic principles (or between Nature and Art, as these are referred to in much of his Empedocles corpus). Although the situation of tragedy remains, for him, constant, how the tragic is understood within this situation does not. Whereas Hegel's philosophy of tragedy develops, elaborates, and maintains a firm theoretical basis, Hölderlin, in an agonized labor of thought, calls into question and subverts aspects of the speculative matrix of tragedy that he had himself elaborated in texts such as "Concerning the Tragic," "Ground for Empedocles," and "The Fatherland in Decline." The task this Epilogue sets itself will therefore be to mark out, in retrospect, the path, with its way-stations and turnings, of Hölderlin's tragic thought.

Hölderlin's tragic protagonist, Empedocles, is a figure who has reached sublime heights of spiritual (as well as intellectual and artistic) self-development. The First and Second Versions stress that, to achieve this realization, and to be able to exercise the beneficent powers in which it found expression, he had to repudiate all human guidance and entrust himself solely and directly to the pure primordial elements of Nature. Although his situation within an epochal crisis and transition is not explicitly thematized in the first two versions, it bespeaks itself in his break with all the philosophical and religious thought-forms available to him and in his direct communion with the pure elemental energies (ultimately the sheer energy of light) from which flows the mature ethically and socially transformative or even revolutionary vision expressed in his final testament.

Although Empedocles is a figure from antiquity, Hölderlin situates him on the threshold of modernity; and his hybristic transgression (encouraged by the very distance that separates him from his own people and from its religious functionaries) is the peculiarly modern one of the self-exaltation of subjectivity (which shatters the cosmic differential unity he had affirmed). In this spirit, Empedocles not only proclaims or accepts the divinization of his own person, but also desacralizes Nature by his quest for mastery; and he perverts the poetic word that should have been his offering to Nature into the supposed ground of Nature's spiritual life.

Although there are already indications, in the first two versions, that the protagonist's fundamental *hybris* lies in his seeking to encompass, in his own singular indivduality, the differential whole of Nature (so as to accomplish a reconciliation of the warring aorgic and organic principles) and that his singular self must therefore be destroyed, this thought is not as yet clearly articulated. Empedocles' self-immolation therefore constitutes an act of atonement, self-purification, and reunion with "all-transforming Nature," more than a genuine sacrifice that would be called for by an imminent turning of the times. Moreover, Hölderlin puts into the mouth of his character Delia a challenge to the sacrificial or death-embracing enthusiasm of Empedocles and his intimates in the name of the inherent validity and beauty of mortal life in its finitude. There are thus from the outset two voices that contest each other in his dramatization of the self-sacrifice of an exceptional, transgressive individual caught up in an epochal transition. One can perhaps say that they enunciate a "double prescription."

In the Third Version and the body of essays connected with it, Empedocles is a tragic figure in that he, as a man of exceptional gifts, has been born into a time, culture, and place in which the aorgic and organic forces manifest their "highest antagonism," and in that he feels called upon to reconcile them, so as to benefit his people. Hölderlin's tragic thought here remains under the Hegelian aegis of reconciliation. Although Empedocles succeeds remarkably in reconciling the warring forces in his concrete and sensuous individuality, this reconciliation must necessarily and immediately disintegrate; for "the sacred spirit of life" cannot be held captive and immobilized in singularity. His own singular existence must therefore be destroyed, so that, in this sense, his death does now constitute a sacrifice demanded by the destiny of the time.

In keeping with the speculative schema, dissolution here ushers in the promise of a "more beautiful" reconciliation to come, one in which the opposites, which interpenetrated one another to the point of in-difference in the

Empedoclean reconciliation, are held together without compromising their incommensurable differences. Moreover, in rendering the dissolution of the singular "ideal," recollection integrates it into "the infinite feeling of life," so that it opens unto novel possibilities and becomes a creative, rather than a destructive, event.

In considering this stage of Hölderlin's tragic thought, at which he takes pains to refine the speculative matrix of tragedy with a focus on the sacrificial role of the singular in an epochal transition, one can agree with Schürmann that he valorizes the destruction of singularity. However, sacrificial destruction is not tantamount to a "tragic denial" of what resists assimilation by a hegemonic phantasm. Hölderlin thinks it rather as the voluntary self-sacrifice of a Chosen One whose destinal role is unique. The speculative-tragic paradigm, dialectically elaborated, merges here with a messianic thought-structure. Hölderlin does not otherwise seek to suppress the singular, but rather opposes its totalizing self-maximization.

In the Third Version, nevertheless, Hölderlin shows himself preoccupied with the idea of a historically demanded and salutary sacrificial death, so that the questioning and restraining voice of Delia, affirming the "mild light" of the mortal condition, is no longer heard. It will, however, make itself heard again, more forcefully and in detachment from Delia's name, in Hölderlin's "Remarks" on Sophoclean tragedy.

In Hölderlin's "Remarks on Oedipus," the very possibility of a unitive reconciliation is rejected. The longed-for union, between nature's power (*die Naturmacht*), or divinity, and man would mark a break in the course of history and an eclipse of memory. The "furious" quest for a "limitless union" must therefore be purified by "limitless separation."

In the character of Oedipus, the aorgic passion of "furious excess" (*zorniges Unmass*) takes the form of bringing to light and rendering manifest what destiny has hidden, and thus of seeking to become one with the god (Apollo) *in knowledge*. Oedipus, however, seeks also, ineffectually, to protect himself from this elemental power which "tragically transposes man from his sphere of life, the midpoint of his inner life . . . and pulls him into the eccentric sphere of the dead."[2] He thus strives "insanely" for full self-consciousness, or for (organically) defining the boundaries of his individuality, seeking to integrate his present reality and the unfolding future with his hidden beginnings.

To depart briefly from Hölderlin, this quest for a unifying self-consciousness recalls Oedipus's answer to the riddle of the sphinx, an answer that grasped together her encrypted characterizations of the stages of human life under the one concept, "man." Significantly, she encrypted them in a counting of feet. Had Oedipus, named for his swollen feet, been willing to pick up on the hints concerning this infirmity (which, however, he strenuously disregarded), he would have had a clue as to his origin—at the cost of shattering the hoped-for integration of his present self with his unknown provenance.

Like Empedocles, Oedipus, as Hölderlin understands him, is a figure caught up in a turning of the times; but the turning, in his case, is not salvific but inaugurates the Hesperian and modern hegemonic principle of self-consciousness. Whereas his inability to rein in his passion betrays his Greek natal affinity to the aorgic element, the form this excess takes is the peculiarly modern one of a "quest for a consciousness." Such liminality is characteristic of Hölderlin's tragic protagonists, whereas Hegel situates the protagonists of Greek tragedy squarely *within* classical ethicality.

Oedipus's self-blinding when he comes face to face with unbearable truth, is also a figure of the loss of the very possibility of a unitive vision that would, so to speak, hold it all together, harmonizing the beginning with what is unfolding now. The darkness that he so strenuously strove to penetrate is what encloses him now. When the god and man turn away from each other in mutual abandonment—or in a faithless "forgetting" which is, in Hölderlin's (itself memorable) understatement, "most easily remembered"—the god reveals himself as sheer time, incapable of coherence or *telos*. Man, for his part, can then no longer unify his own life, as Oedipus had sought to do. He finds himself exposed to irremediable discordance; and the impact of being thrown back, in the extremity of suffering, upon the empty forms of time and space frustrates any further effort to accomplish a speculative conversion of the negative.

In faithlessly turning away from the god, the human being nevertheless does so "in a sacred manner;" for, given that the human condition, as the condition of mortality, is inherently singularizing, the "eccentric enthusiasm" (so called because it tears the human being away from its own "midpoint") that seeks a union destructive of singularity reveals itself as a passion for death, which needs to be purified. This purification is now the essential work of tragedy, wrested free of both the speculative and the sacrificial distortions of the tragic paradigm.

In *Antigone*, on Hölderlin's interpretation, the tragic conflict brings a fully formed epochal configuration—which has, however, become rigid and ossified—into confrontation with a subversive but still formless challenge, or with what, in Schürmann's terms, one could call the "withdrawing undertow." This challenge confronts a self-absolutizing principle (here Kreon's absolutization of rulership and of oppositional identifications, such as patriot and traitor) with the radical finitude of the mortal condition which erodes all absolutes. Not only does Antigone recognize that no instituted principles can pretend to hegemony in the "unseen" domain (Hades), but the subversive impact of her recognition is heightened in that its concrete focus is emphatically finite and singular: a determination to give at least symbolic burial to one dishonored corpse, that of a brother who, given the history of the "house," is strictly irreplaceable. As concerns the seeming disproportion between the force of her passion and its object, a rotting corpse (note that Sophocles emphasizes its repellent putrefaction), Hölderlin comments astutely:

> That which is, in keeping with the tragic, temporally exhausted—the object of which is after all not really of interest to the heart—follows the tearing spirit of the time most excessively, and this [spirit] then appears wild . . . it is unsparing, as the spirit of the ever-living un-written wilderness and the world of the dead.[3]

Antigone recognizes "the spirit of the highest" as being apart from law (*gesetzlos*); and it pulls her into an "unlettered wilderness" because it does not offer any countervailing principle or body of laws (the "unwritten laws" that she appeals to are precisely that: they are unformulated and incapable of grounding an epochal nomic configuration). In this sense, *Antigone* is, for Hölderlin, a tragedy of epochal dys-limitation (*Entgrenzung*), or of the nomic erosion of the *patria*.

Hölderlin does discern, in the finitizing force of the "natal turning," the promise of a salutary ethical and political transformation. In "a more humane time," a new democratic and libertarian form of government (closely akin to Spinoza's vision in the *Theologico-Political Treatise*),[4] and a new solicitude for what would today be called the biosphere, can ensue. However, the "more humane time" still remains elusive; and one must today question the distorted tragic, salvific, and (self)sacrificial structure of thought that seems to inspire global terrorism. If tragedy has, in the wake of the horrors of recent and contemporary world history, lost its viability as a literary form, it has not lost its relevance as a thought-structure to be critically examined and questioned as to its import.

In this context, Hölderlin's effort to wrest tragedy free of its sacrificial and speculative construals retains its importance. Hölderlin himself recognizes two injunctions that spring from the tragic knowledge of discordant temporalization, or from what Schürmann calls "the legislative-transgressive fracture." The first of these calls for "a firm abiding before the changing time," which Hölderlin also characterizes as "a heroic hermit's life" and as "highest consciousness" (taking the place of the differential reconciliation that was accorded a similar epithet in "The General Ground" of the Empedocles corpus).[5] This firm abiding is not any sort of restrictive self-entrenchment, nor yet resignation, but rather a conduct of life that takes its measure from discordant temporalization and thus refuses allegiance to any absolutizing or totalizing maximizations.

The second injunction is to turn toward, rather than away from, the finitude of the mortal condition, contrary to what Hölderlin calls "the eternal tendency" toward aorgic excess. Its force is to offer resistance to "eccentric enthusiasm" in all it forms; and Hölderlin considered such resistance to be the guiding concern of his work on tragedy.

These two injunctions are not disjointed, but intimately complement and require one another. It was their import and urgency that, in the end, motivated Hölderlin to transpose Sophoclean tragedy into a language, conceptuality, and form of poetic presentation that, he hoped, would speak to modernity.

To conclude on a gentler reflective note, however, than the memory of the stark tragic protagonists of antiquity, or the evocation of the traumas of modernity, here, in translation, are Hölderlin's own words ending his hymn, *The Archipelago*:

> But you, immortal, even though Greek song may now not
> Celebrate you, as once, out of your billows, oh sea-god!
> My soul still often resounds, so that, above the waters,
> Alert without fear, spirit may train, like the swimmer,
> In the fresh joy of the strong ones, and divine speech understand
> Change and becoming, and when tearing time
> Too forcefully seizes my head, and affliction and errance
> Among mortals shake up my own mortal life,
> Let me then remain mindful of stillness within your depths.[6]

Notes

PROLOGUE

Epigraph from Marc Froment-Meurice, "'Aphasia' the Last Word," trans. Anne O'Byrne in *Philosophy and Tragedy*, ed. Miguel de Beistegui and Simon Sparks (London: Routledge, 2000), 221–38 (223).

1. Françoise Dastur, *Hölderlin: le retournement natal* (Fougères, Versanne: encre marine, 1997). This book incorporates the author's earlier *Hölderlin: tragédie et modernité*, published by the same press in 1992 and now out of print, together with the new "Nature et poésie."

2. This term, now generally used, really needs to be problematized for the way it conceals an advance selection of the figures or texts that will then be drawn upon to define a historical epoch and culture.

CHAPTER ONE. THE TRAGIC TURNING AND TRAGIC PARADIGM IN PHILOSOPHY

Epigraph from Reiner Schürmann, *Des hégémonies brisées* (Mauvezin: Trans-Euro-Repress, 1996), 774.

1. Following the *Pantheismusstreit* or "pantheism conflict" that ensued when Jacobi claimed, in *Ueber die Lehre des Spinoza in Briefen an den Herrn Moses Mendelsohn* of 1785, that Lessing had confided to him his own Spinozism, the way was open for what Pierre-François Moreau characterizes as a rival doctrine of divinity, consummated in German Idealism. See here P.-F. Moreau, "Spinoza's Reception and Influence," trans. Roger Ariew in *The Cambridge Companion to Spinoza*, ed. Don Garrett (Cambridge: Cambridge University Press, 1996), 408–33. Notwithstanding the importance of Spinoza's thought for German Romanticism and Idealism, however, Hölderlin, for the most part, does not address it; and his exaltation and divinization of the great elements of nature in his fragmentary *The Death of Empedocles* is indebted, not to Spinoza's *Deus sive Natura*, but to the Empedoclean elemental "roots" (*rhizomata*), which resonated with the poet's own near-mystical experience of nature in

early life. However, Hölderlin had read Spinoza; and the scholar who has painstakingly researched and interpreted this intellectual relationship, Margarethe Wegenast, finds the mark of Spinoza's thought in *Hyperion*. See her *Hölderlins Spinoza-Rezeption, und ihre Bedeutung für die Konzeption des "Hyperion"* (Tübingen: Niemeyer, 1990).

2. Miguel de Beistegui and Simon Sparks, "Introduction" to their edited volume, *Philosophy and Tragedy* (London: Routledge, 2000), 1–9. Dennis J. Schmidt, *On Germans and Other Greeks: Tragedy and Ethical Life* (Bloomington: Indiana University Press, 2001) echoes this thought. See his chapter "Kant and Schelling."

3. For a concise discussion, see Peter Szondi, "The Notion of the Tragic in Schelling, Hölderlin, and Hegel," in *On Textual Understanding, and Other Essays*, trans. Harvey Mendelsohn, (Minneapolis: University of Minnesota Press, 1986), 43–55.

4. Martha C. Nussbaum, in *The Fragility of Goodness: Luck and Ethics in Greek Tragedy and Philosophy* (Cambridge: Cambridge University Press, 1986) pays particular attention to Euripides' *Hecuba*. Hölderlin is the only one among the German Idealist thinkers to devote some appreciative attention to Euripides, mostly in the form of short translations.

5. See Plato, *Rep.*, 607b-608a.

6. I outline this history in my "Hölderlin, Johannn Christian Friedrich," *The Edinburgh Encyclopedia of Modern Theory and Criticism*, ed. Julian Wolfreys (Edinburgh: Edinburgh University Press, 2002), 29–36.

7. See note to chapter epigraph, above.

8. D. J. Schmidt, *op. cit.*, 80. Schmidt provides a translation of Schelling's Tenth Letter as Appendix B, 86–88.

9. Letter 118, 24 February 1796, SW III, 224–26.

10. For detailed references to SW II, see chs. 1 and 3, above.

11. G. W. F. Hegel, "Über die wissenschaftlichen Behandlungsarten des Naturrechts . . . ," *Werke*, II, 434–530. Both Szondi in *op. cit.* and Miguel de Beistegui in "Hegel on the Tragedy of Thinking," in *Philosophy and Tragedy*, 11–37, stress the origin of Hegel's philosophy of tragedy in his early theological writings (where, however, tragedy is not explicitly referred to). This wider interpretive perspective cannot be taken up within the compass of this chapter.

12. G. W. F. Hegel, *Phänomenologie des Geistes*, *Werke*, III, and *Vorlesungen über die Aesthetik*, III, *Werke*, XV.

13. Szondi, *op. cit.*, 49. Compare here Hegel's own summary, *Werke*, II, 509.

14. *Werke*, II, 494.

15. *Werke*, II, 495.

16. See F. Hölderlin, "Anmerkungen zur Antigonä," SW II, 913–21, and the fuller discussion in ch. 6 in this book.

17. On the issue of comedy (which remained of concern to Hegel but did not interest Hölderlin), see Rodolphe Gasché, "Self-Dissolving Seriousness: On the Comic in the Hegelian Conception of Tragedy," in de Beistegui and Sparks, *op. cit.*, 38–52.

18. *Werke*, II, 496.

19. G. W. F. Hegel, *Phänomenologie des Geistes*, *Werke*, III, 327–54 and 529–44.

20. *Werke*, III, 348.

21. De Beistegui, *op. cit.*, 21.

22. Klaus Düsing, "Die Theorie der Tragödie bei Hölderlin und Hegel," in Jamme and Pöggeler, eds., *Jenseits des Idealismus*, 55–82 (75).

23. *Werke*, III, 339; see also 536.

24. *Werke*, III, 332.

25. *Werke*, III, 333.

26. *Ibid.* See Tina Chanter, "Antigone's Dilemma," in *Re-Reading Levinas*, ed. R. Bernasconi and S. Critchley (Bloomington: Indiana University Press, 1991), 130–46, for an astute analysis of the interdependence of divine and civic law in Hegel's reading of *Antigone*.

27. F. Hölderlin, "Anmerkungen zur Antigonä," SW II, 918.

28. *Werke*, III, 354.

29. *Werke*, III, 349.

30. For a discussion of tragedy's situation between epic and comedy in Hegel, see D. J. Schmidt, *op. cit.*, 104–10.

31. *Werke*, III, 536.

32. Friedrich Nietzsche, *Die Geburt der Tragödie aus dem Geiste der Musik*; Giorgio Colli and Mazzino Montinari, *Friedrich Nietzsche: Sämtliche Werke; Kritische Studienausgabe*, vol. I, 11–156. See section 7. Nietzsche (in dialogue with Schiller) interprets the original tragic chorus as a satyr chorus and comments that "the satyr, as a fictive being of nature, stands in the same relation to the man of culture as Dionysian music to civilization" (55). The satyr chorus was in fact one of the three choral types that evolved from the original circle dance performed at the Athenian Dionysia, the other two being the tragic and comic choruses.

33. For Hegel, it is precisely the supposed passivity and disempowerment of the tragic chorus that renders it generative of the tragic emotions. See *Werke*, III, 636f.

34. *Werke*, III, 537.

35. *Werke*, III, 540. Hegel's grammar, in the concluding sentence, is somewhat elliptical.

36. Letter 246, 2 April 1804, SW III, 472f. This is Hölderlin's last letter to Wilmans and, except for a few words to Princess Auguste of Hesse-Homburg, the last letter of his lucidity. Pöggeler, in "Die engen Schranken . . . ," also cites part of this passage.

37. See *Werke*, XV, 480 and 522.

38. *Werke*, XV, 523f.

39. *Werke*, XV, 526.

40. *Werke*, XV, 525f.

41. *Werke*, XV, 537f.

42. *Werke*, XV, 534, 538. See, however, his more sympathetic treatment of "The Oriental Epic" at 395–400.

43. *Werke*, XV, 540.

44. *Werke*, XV, 550.

45. See *Werke*, XV, 567.

46. See "Die dionysische Weltanschauung," "Die Geburt des tragischen Gedankens," and "Sokrates und die griechische Tragödie," in *Sämtliche Werke; Kritische Studienausgabee* (to be referred to as SW/KS), I, 511–640. For a detailed discussion of Nietzsche's texts on tragedy, see John Sallis, *Crossings: Nietzsche and the Space of Tragedy* (Chicago: University of Chicago Press, 1991).

47. See this work, ch. 6, below, for further reference to Burckhardt, as well as D. J. Schmidt's comments, *op. cit.*, 192f.

48. See *Nachgelassene Fragmente, 1869–1874*, SW/KS, VII, 233–37, and "Die Philosophie im tragischen Zeitalter der Griechen," SW/KS, I, 801–72. See here David Farrell Krell's detailed and insightful discussion in his *Lunar Voices: Of Tragedy, Poetry, Fiction, and Thought* (Chicago: University of Chicago Press, 1995), 1–45.

49. "Versuch einer Selbstkritik," SW/KS, I, 20. Nietzsche comments similarly in the section of *Ecce Homo* that addresses *The Birth of Tragedy*. Concerning the whole question of the musical rebirth of tragedy, see D. J. Schmidt's discussion in *op. cit.*, ch. 5. For a discussion of the question of whether Nietzsche's *Thus Spoke Zarathustra* can be considered as the (philosophical and poetic) rebirth of tragedy, see Walter Brogan, "The Tragic Figure of the Last Philosopher," in *Philosophy and Tragedy*, 152–66.

50. Schmidt stresses and discusses this need in *op. cit.*, ch. 5.

51. "Die Geburt der Tragödie" (henceforth GT), section 11, SW/KS, I, 75.

52. "Versuch einer Selbstkritik," SW/KS, I, 13.

53. GT, section 12, SW/KS, I, 83. The "demon" presumably alludes to Socrates' *daimonion*, which Nietzsche discusses in GT.

54. SW/KS, I, 12.

55. The phrase ("die Innigkeit des Streites") is Heidegger's in his "Der Ursprung des Kunstwerkes," Holzwege, 4th ed. (Frankfurt a.M.: Klostermann, 1963), 7–65 (38). It would be illuminating to consider this Heideggerian strife between Earth and World, instigated by the work of art, in its relation to the Hölderlinian strife between the aorgic and organic principles, as well as to Nietzsche's strife between the Dionysian and Apollonian energies, and perhaps even to Schürmann's understanding of how tragedy brings to the fore *le différend*.

56. SW/KS, I, 13, 19.

57. SW/KS, I, 12.

58. Nietzsche's allusion in speaking of "the forceful effort to train one's eyes on the sun" (GT, section 9, SW/KS, I, 65) is evidently to the Platonic ascent from the

cave in *Rep.* VII. For a discussion of this ascent, see my *Vision's Invisibles: Philosophical Explorations* (Albany: State University of New York Press, 2003), ch. 2.

59. *Ibid.*

60. SW/KS, I, 18.

61. SW/KS, I, 17f and 47.

62. GT, section 4, SW/KS, 39.

63. GT, section 3, SW/KS, I, 38.

64. GT, section 4, SW/KS, I, 42.

65. Günter Figal, "Aesthetically Limited Reason: on Nietzsche's *The Birth of Tragedy*," trans. John Protevi and Peter Poellner, *Philosophy and Tragedy*, 139–51 (141, 147).

66. D. F. Krell, *Lunar Voices*, 20.

67. GT, section 9, SW/KS, I, 66f.

68. GT, section 9, SW/KS, I, 69–71.

69. See the cited pages of GT, 9. The last statement is on p. 69. On Nietzsche and the question of race, see Schmidt, *op. cit.*, 218f. Schmidt focuses on the notion of "the German," rather than on Nietzsche's conception of the "Aryan" and "Semitic" identities. A study devoted to the latter would also have to address his recognition of an "Aryan" and "Semitic" duality *within the Greek cultural heritage*, as well as his use of the normative term "Aryan" (from the Sanskrit *arya*, meaning "noble") as the counterpart of the purely classificatory (Latin-derived) term "Semitic," and the restriction of the latter's quite expansive range (comprising, for instance, the Arabic, Assyrian, and Ethiopian peoples and languages) to the Judaic.

70. GT, section 9, SW/KS, 69.

71. See this work, ch. 7, below, for references and discussion.

72. Heidegger, *Einführung*, 81. The Hölderlin citation is from "In lieblicher Bläue . . ." ("In lovely blueness . . ."), SW I, 479–81. This text is transmitted only as part of Wilhelm Waiblinger's 1825 novel *Phaeton*, which is based on the figure of Hölderlin, and for which he drew on his close acquaintance with the poet and access to his papers during the latter's mental illness. The editors of SW comment that it is impossible to determine to what extent he faithfully renders Hölderlin's own words (SW I, 1095).

73. D. J. Schmidt, *op. cit.*, ch. 6. For a more critically focused discussion of the rectoral address than Schmidt's (who reads it in the spirit of Gadamer's comparison of Heidegger's political involvement to that of Plato in Syracuse), see David Farrell Krell, *Daimon Life: Heidegger and Life Philosophy* (Bloomington: Indiana University Press, 1992), 142–47.

74. Heidegger, *Einführung*, 83. Heidegger italicizes the first occurrence of *Irre*.

75. M. Heidegger, "Vom Wesen der Wahrheit," *Wegmarken*, 73–98, and *Parmenides*, GA, 54.

76. See section 5b.

77. M. Heidegger, *Holzwege*, 4th ed. (Frankfurt a.M.: Klostermann, 1963), 248–95.

78. O. Pöggeler, "Die engen Schranken . . . ," 28. Heidegger's *Beiträge zur Philosophie. Vom Ereignis* is published as GA, 65. I have kept Pöggeler's plural, referring to *Beiträge* (*Contributions*), even though in English the work would normally be referred to in the singular.

79. M. Heidegger, "Der Spruch des Anaximander," *Holzwege*, 296–343 (339). The Greek phrase would ordinarily translate as "to give justice . . . [in compensation] for injustice;" but such an ordinary translation will not be Heidegger's.

80. "The Saying," 310f. Heidegger explicitly dissociates *epochē* from its Husserlian methodic meaning as the deliberate suspension of the thetic act of consciousness. It is being itself that, as it were, suspends or conceals itself in every granting of manifestation, thus inviting oblivion.

81. "The Saying," 328.

82. "The Saying," 330.

83. "The Saying," 334.

84. R. Schürmann, *Des hégémonies brisées*. On p. 28, Schürmann writes that "if life nourishes itself from common meanings, that which passes as its other, death, is signified for us by the singular. Hölderlin situates the good in the unanimous, in the unity which unifies; and in the singular he situates "the root of all evil." The reference is to Hölderlin's "Die Wurzel alles Übels," a two-line poetic fragment dating from 1798–1900 (SW I, 222), which hardly forms a sufficient textual basis for Schürmann's judgment. See also his brief further references to Hölderlin at p. 68, n. 45, and p. 741, with p. 771, n. 86.

85. See Part III, ch. 2, of *Des hégémonies brisées*, as well as Schürmann's *Heidegger on Being and Acting: From Principles to Anarchy*, trans. Christine-Marie Gros (Bloomington: Indiana University Press, 1987).

86. Simon Sparks, "Fatalities: Freedom and the Question of Language in Walter Benjamin's Reading of Tragedy," *Philosophy and Tragedy*, 193–218 (212).

87. *Des hégémonies*, 30.

88. *Des hégémonies*, 49.

89. *Des hégémonies*, 37. Concerning *deinon*, see this work, ch. 7, below.

CHAPTER TWO. COMMUNING WITH THE PURE ELEMENTS: THE FIRST TWO VERSIONS OF *THE DEATH OF EMPEDOCLES*

Epigraph from Rosalind Krauss, "The /Cloud/," in *Agnes Martin*, ed. Barbara Haskell (New York: Harry N. Abrams, 1992), 155.

1. Letter 179, SW III, 351–53. References are given to SW rather than to the earlier *Grosse* and *Kleine* Stuttgart edition, or to the critical Frankfurt edition (see the

Bibliography for details), since it embodies the latest textual scholarship and also offers extensive scholarly commentaries.

2. Letter 180, SW III, 354–60.

3. Letter 196, SW III, 395–97.

4. See SW II, 421–24.

5. Hölderlin's key source for the life of Empedocles was Diogenes Laërtius. For a detailed discussion of his scholarly sources, see the editors' comments at SW II, 1097, and Uvo Hölscher, *Empedokles und Hölderlin* (Frankfurt a.M.: Insel Verlag, 1965), ch. 1. Hölscher stresses, apart from Diogenes Laërtius, the importance of Henricus Stephanus (also known as Henri Ėtienne), *Poesis Philosophica* (1573), and Ralph Cudworth, *Systema intellectuale huius mundi* (1680), while the editors of SW also cite evidence of Hölderlin's use of Georg Christoph Hamberger, *Nachrichten von den vornehmsten Schriftstellern vom Anfang der Welt bis 1500* (Part I, 1756), and Jacob Brücker, *Historia critica philosophiae*, which was published in six volumes, beginning in 1742.

6. SW II, 421.

7. Wolfgang Riedel, "*Deus seu Natura*: Wissensgeschichtliche Motive einer religionsgeschichtlichen Wende—im Blick auf Hölderlin," *Hölderlin-Jahrbuch* 31 (1998/99): 171–203 (174).

8. Riedel, *op. cit.*, 189. On Jacobi (as well as Wegenast), see ch. 1, n. 2. See Hölderlin, "Zu Jacobis Briefen über die Lehre des Spinoza," SW II, 492–95.

9. SW II, 293. Consider here C. M. Bowra's comment on Pindar, a poet whom Hölderlin was intensely fascinated with and some of whose Odes he translated: "Pindar's guiding and central theme is the part of experience in which human beings are exalted or illumined by a divine force, and this he commonly compares with light. At such times the consciousness is marvellously enhanced . . ." *The Odes of Pindar*, trans. C. M. Bowra (Harmondsworth: Penguin, 1985), xcv.

10. SW II, 280.

11. SW II, 286, note.

12. SW II, 299. Nietzsche's characterization of the figure of the priest as embodying the spirit of *ressentiment* may well be indebted to his reading of *The Death of Empedocles*.

13. SW II, 333.

14. SW II, 330. The emphasis on purification (*Erläuterung*) hearkens back to Empedocles' philosophical poem *Katharmoi* (*Purifications*).

15. SW II, 349.

16. SW II, 354.

17. Plato, *Phaedo*, 115e. Socrates' indifference contrasts markedly with the Greek emphasis on burial rites, which finds expression in Sophocles' *Antigone*.

18. SW II, 353.

19. Plato, *Phaedrus*, 230d.

20. SW II, 354. It is striking that, in contrast to Socrates' disdain for trees and the countryside, Hölderlin's Empedocles expresses particular veneration for "the unerring trees" of his ancestral garden, whereas he feels estranged from the "people in the city" whom Socrates favored.

21. See SW II, 347f.

22. SW II, 494.

23. Riedel, *op. cit.*, 188.

24. SW II, 342. Hölderlin is often portrayed as waiting for the absconded gods only in renunciation; and what he may have understood by their advent tends to be considered enigmatic. This passage is of special interest in relation to this question, since Empedocles here actually welcomes the advent of the gods.

25. SW II, 343.

26. See the discussion by the editors of SW, who point out that "the enterprises of the [French] Directorate, as to foreign policy, were not intended to extend the Revolution, but to gain power and annex German territory." SW II, 1101.

27. SW II, 393. The text cited here forms part of Hölderlin's *Reinschrift* (definitive version) of the opening section of act 1, scene 1.

28. SW II, 363, 392.

29. This figure echoes the biblical parable of the sower (*Mark IV*, 13–20), as well as Plato's discussion of the philosophically gifted nature that grows up stunted, having been sown into a soil that cannot nourish it (*Rep.*, 429a).

30. SW II, 394.

31. *Ibid.*

32. Françoise Dastur, *Dire le temps: esquisse d'une chrono-logie phénoménologique* (Fougères, La Versanne: encre marine, 1994), 26. Dastur notes, with reference to the Sanskrit grammarian Pāṇini, (5th cent. B.C.E.), that a privileging of the name or noun is by no means unavoidable in the study of Indogermanic languages: Pāṇini's grammar "rests upon the principle of the verbal phrase, the center of which is the verb, to which [*auxquels*, referring to both verb and phrase] all the other factors of the action (agent, instrument, object, and so on) are referred in the same way" (*Dire le temps*, 25, n. 7).

33. *Hölderlin to Hegel*, 26 January, 1995, Letter 95; SW III, 175–77 (176). Hölderlin had attended Fichte's lectures in Jena, from where he was writing. He remarks, however, that he had noted down these thoughts while still in Waltershausen, where he had read Fichte's "first pages," right after reading Spinoza; and he adds tantalizingly that "Fichte confirmed for me . . . ," without completing the sentence.

34. SW II, 380.

35. SW II, 386f.

36. SW II, 387.

37. SW II, 348. Delia's lines here (". . . und heften / Die Augen an Bleibendes" [". . . and fix / Their eyes on what abides"]) resonate in the penultimate verse of Hölderlin's late hymn *Andenken*: "Und die Lieb' auch heftet fleissig die Augen" ("And love also diligently fixes its eyes").

38. *Ibid.*

39. Hölderlin, *Hyperion*, SW II, 92. The novel was published in two volumes in 1796 and 1798. Dennis J. Schmidt offers a detailed discussion of *Hyperion* in relation to *The Death of Empedocles* in ch. 4 of *op. cit*.

40. Preface to *Hyperion*, SW II, 13.

41. The "Fragment of Hyperion," representing an earlier stage of the epistolary novel, was published in Friedrich Schiller's literary periodical *Neue Thalia* in 1793. See SW II, 177.

42. *Ibid.*

43. SW II, 91.

CHAPTER THREE. SINGULARITY AND RECONCILIATION: THE THIRD VERSION OF *THE DEATH OF EMPEDOCLES*

Epigraph from Friedrich Hölderlin, "Über den Unterschied der Dichtarten" ("Concerning the Difference Among Poetic Modes"), SW II, 553–59 [555]. This essay is generally taken to date, like most of the Empedocles complex, from Hölderlin's first Homburg period.

1. SW II, 425–59. Hölderlin himself left the essay untitled; the title "Concerning the Tragic" ("Über das Tragische") was chosen by the editors of SW. Earlier editions often use the section title 'Ground for Empedocles' as the title of the entire body of essays.

2. SW II, 440–48, and 397–417.

3. SW II, 446–51, and 444f. In earlier editions, the essay is titled "Becoming in Perishing" and is not included in the Empedocles corpus. The editors of SW justify its inclusion on the basis of both manuscript evidence and thought content. All the texts from "Concerning the Tragic" to the final "Project" date from the fall and winter of 1799/1800.

4. The Third Version breaks off with a fragment of the first choral ode.

5. See SW II, 701–64. The editors comment that Hölderlin's purpose in these translations—or linguistic transpositions—was to study Pindar's diction and rhythm, irrespective of the requirements of the German language (SW II, 1289). In 1798, Hölderlin also translated two of the odes of Horace.

6. I quote from the article "Ode" by Stephen F. Fogle and Paul H. Fry in *The New Princeton Encyclopedia of Poetry and Poetics*, ed. A. Preminger and D. V. F. Brogan (New York: MJF Books, 1993), 855–57.

7. SW II, 425.

8. Hölderlin appears to have had in mind the contemporary tragic poet, given that, for the Greek tragedians, the Homeric epics and myths that they drew on were neither alien nor remote.

9. Hölderlin here introduces this term, which will be important in the context of his "Remarks" on Sophoclean tragedy.

10. SW II, 428.

11. The terms "aorgic" (the primordially unformed and anarchic) and "organic" (what is articulated, ordered, individualized), which remain crucial for Hölderlin's thought, make their appearance here and play against the more conventionally named opposites, Art and Nature. There is an evident kinship between these Hölderlinian notions and Nietzsche's Dionysian and Apollonian art energies (which issue from nature) in his *The Birth of Tragedy*.

12. SW II, 429. The phrase is repeated.

13. SW II, 430. Hölderlin's emphasis.

14. In the Empedocles corpus, Hölderlin does not challenge the quest for reconciliation which characterizes, in particular, Hegel's analysis of Greek tragedy. Compare here Miguel de Beistegui, "Hegel or the Tragedy of Thinking," *Philosophy and Tragedy*, 11–37.

15. SW II, 431f. Consider again here the similarity between Hölderlin's argumentation and that of Heidegger concerning the intimacy of strife between, to use Hölderlin's terms, aorgic Earth and organic World in "Der Ursprung des Kunstwerkes" ("The Origin of the Work of Art").

16. Friedrich Nietzsche, *Die Geburt der Tragödie*, SW/KS, I, 9–156.

17. SW II, 433.

18. SW II, 438.

19. See Letters 128 and 129 to G. W. F. Hegel, SW III, 243–45.

20. *Hölderlin to Neuffer*, 16 February 1797, Letter 137, SW III, 258–60 (259).

21. SW II, 438f.

22. SW II, 676–81. For a discussion of Euripides' *Hecuba*, see Martha C. Nussbaum, *The Fragility of Goodness: Luck and Ethics in Greek Tragedy and Philosophy* (Cambridge: Cambridge University Press, 1986), ch. 13.

23. His talk of wings and flight feathers obviously alludes to Plato's *Phaedrus*, as does the later reference to the "flowery Ilissus."

24. SW II, 398f.

25. SW II, 404.

26. Compare Plato, *Phdr.*, 256b–e.

27. SW II, 409.

28. SW II, 412.

29. SW II, 414.

30. As noted earlier, Hölderlin had suggested that Manes was an apparition or *revenant* rather than a living person; so Empedocles' (revoked) invitation to him to join him in death is less than consistent.

31. Miguel de Beistegui, "Hegel or the Tragedy of Thinking," *Philosophy and Tragedy*, 12.

32. SW II, 446–51. See note 3 above for discussion.

33. SW II, 446. I translate both Hölderlin's *besonderes* and *einzelnes* as "singular." His own use of these terms does not support translating the first of them as "particular" and only the second as "singular." They are used equivalently, with at most a difference of emphasis.

34. Reiner Schürmann, "Ultimate Double Binds," *The Graduate Faculty Philosophy Journal* 14:2–15:1 (1991): 213–36. A revised version of this essay, translated by Kathleen Blamey, appears in *Heidegger Toward the Turn: Essays on the Work of the 1930s*, ed. James Risser (Albany: State University of New York Press, 1999), 243–67.

35. SW II, 448.

36. SW II, 449.

37. SW II, 450.

38. "Über die verschiedenen Arten zu dichten," SW II, 514–18.

39. Jean-François Courtine, "Of Tragic Metaphor," in *Philosophy and Tragedy*, 59–77 [64f].

40. See here Philippe Lacoue-Labarthe, "La césure du spéculatif," in *L'imitation des modernes: Typographies II* (Paris: Galilée, 1986), 43.

41. SW II, 445. David Farrell Krell, in his *Lunar Voices* (p.18), expresses reservations, on feminist grounds, about Hölderlin's annotations of "naiv idealisch" with respect to Panthea, as well as to Empedocles (later also "heroisch idealisch") in the "Plan for the Third Version" (SW II, 442f). However, these annotations do not refer to the *dramatis personae*, but to the appropriate poetic "tones" of their utterances, in keeping with Hölderlin's discussion in "Vom Wechsel der Töne" ("On the Change of Tones") and "Über den Unterschied der Dichtarten" ("On the Difference of Poetic Modes"), SW II, 524–26 and 553–59.

CHAPTER FOUR.
BETWEEN HÖLDERLIN'S EMPEDOCLES AND EMPEDOCLES OF AKRAGAS

Epigraph from Empedocles, *On Nature* (Περὶ Φύσεως, also translated as *Physics*), Fragment 23 (DK), cited by Simplicius. The translation given is based on the textual construal and translation by M. R. Wright in *Empedocles: The Extant Fragments* (New Haven: Yale University Press, 1981), and on Kathleen Freeman's translation in *Ancilla to the Presocratics* (Cambridge: Harvard University Press, 1971). All fragments will be cited by their Diels-Kranz numbers, and the translations given are indebted to the two sources cited.

1. See ch. 1, n. 6 for details.

2. For details, see Wright, *Empedocles*, 3–17, and Diogenes Laërtius, *Lives of the Philosophers*, trans. and ed. A. Robert Caponigri (Chicago: Regnery, 1969), 59, 61, 64.

3. As to contemporary scholarship, see Wright's discussion, *Empedocles*, 16. Diogenes' accounts include death of unknown causes in the Peloponnesus, death by hanging, death by accident at an advanced age, and transformation into a god.

4. See ch. 2, n. 38 concerning a similar line in the Second Version. This note also gives the reference for the hymn.

5. Jean Bollack, *Empédocle*, vol. III: *Les Origines: Commentaire I* (Paris: Editions de Minuit, 1969), 19–26 [22]. As to life and death being mere names, see, for instance, Fragment 9. The link between scientific knowledge and esoteric powers (as well as the religious and initiatory tone of Fragments 3–5) point to an interconnection between *On Nature* and the religiously focused *Purifications*. Hölderlin grasped this interconnection, as well as the fundamentally religious character of Empedocles' thought—in contrast to an entire tradition of scholarship which, as Wright points out, regards the two works as "incompatible or even contradictory" (*Empedocles*, 57). One can regard the scholarly bewilderment concerning both Fragment 111 and the conjunction between the two poems as corroborating Heidegger's often repeated assertion that, in the Western intellectual tradition, it is technology that called for science (being thus prior in a nonchronological sense), rather than constituting the mere application of science. Empedocles' thought (which Heidegger does not discuss) moves evidently along an ec-centric path in conjoining knowledge of nature, not with technology, but with esoteric powers.

6. See *Lives*, 59.

7. Wright, *Empedocles*, 165.

8. For a table of designations and the fragments in which they occur, see Wright, *Empedocles*, 23.

9. Wright, *Empedocles*, 254. For Empedocles, elemental mixture is not a blending in which the ingredients become indiscernible, but composition governed by *proportion*. He himself offers an analogy with the painter in Fragment 23; but, given the differences between Greek painting (which relied on four unblended colors) and contemporary painterly practice, the analogy of the mosaicist might be more appropriate today. Empedocles' concern for the proportional relationships governing elemental composition was appreciated by Aristotle (see, for instance, *De An.*, 410a4) and was regarded by other ancient commentators, such as Simplicius, as the mark of his Pythagorean heritage.

10. SW II, 293.

11. See, for instance, Tenzin Wangyal Rinpoche, *Healing with Form, Energy, and Light* (Ithaca, NY: Snow Lion Publications, 2002), which comes out of the Tibetan indigenous Bön tradition, and Sogyal Rinpoche, *The Tibetan Book of Living and Dying* (San Francisco: Harper, 1993, 2001), which is written from the perspective of the Nyingmapa School of Tibetan Buddhism and the teachings of Dzogchen. Sogyal Rinpoche discusses the role of the elements in the death process and the "intermediate

state." See also John C. Huntington and Dina Bangdel, *The Circle of Bliss: Buddhist Meditational Art* (Chicago: Serindia Publications, 2003).

12. Friedrich Solmsen, "Love and Strife in Empedocles' Cosmology," in *Studies in Presocratic Philosophy*, vol II, ed. R. E. Allen and David J. Furley (Atlantic Highlands: Humanities Press, 1971), 221–64.

13. He discusses both Fragment 17 and relevant passages from Aristotle's *De gen et corr.* on 238f of the cited essay. Strangely, he writes on 235 that "no passage is preserved which includes the word κύκλος;" yet in Fragment 17 (line 12), the elements are said to be always unmoved as they interact κατὰ κύκλον.

14. A. A. Long, "Empedocles' Cosmic Cycle in the 'Sixties," in *The Pre-Socratics: A Collection of Critical Essays*, 2nd rev. ed., ed. Alexander P. D. Mourelatos (Princeton: Princeton University Press, 1993), 397–425.

15. Long, *op. cit.*, 399.

16. Long, *op. cit.*, 413.

17. SW II, 1189.

18. SW II, 429.

19. Françoise Dastur, "Tragedy and Speculation," in *Philosophy and Tragedy*, 78–87.

20. SW II, 918.

21. See Wright, *Empedocles*, 25, and compare Fragment 62.

22. *Hölderlin to Casimir Ulrich von Böhlendorff*, 4 December 1801, Letter 237, SW II, 459–62 (460).

23. *Ibid.*

24. Charles H. Kahn, "Religion and Philosophy in Empedocles' Doctrine of the Soul," in Mourelatos, ed., *The Pre-Socratics*, 426–56. As Kahn notes (446), his position as to the identity of the *daimōn* agrees in important respects with F. M. Cornford's.

CHAPTER FIVE. THE FAITHLESS TURNING: HÖLDERLIN'S READING OF *OEDIPUS TYRANNOS*

Epigraph from Philippe Lacoue-Labarthe, "La césure du spéculatif," 65.

1. See SW III, 408–74. A list of the letters is given in SW II, 1322f. The editors point out that these are Hölderlin's last letters before mental illness closed in on him. See further *Fritz Horn to Isaac Sinclair*, November 1802 (?), GSA VII: 2, 239.

2. These include an earlier partial translation of the first choral ode of the *Antigone*, part of the first *stasimon* of *Oedipus at Colonus* (which dates from an earlier period, 1796), as well as of the opening verses of that tragedy (1802) and parts of *Ajax* (which he particularly loved, and which is significant for his late hymn *Mnemosyne*). See SW II, 691, 776f, and 778–81. See here Bernhard Böschenstein, "'Oedipus auf Colonus' in Hölderlins Dichtung, Übersetzung, und Tragödientheorie," *Hölderlin*

Jahrbuch 31 (1998/90): 162–67. This summary of the researches carried out by a study group presents important insights concerning the relationship, for Hölderlin, between this Sophoclean tragedy and his hymn *Der Rhein*, and between the figures of the aged Oedipus, Rousseau, Empedocles, and Hölderlin himself: "all are the precursors of a new time, all stand at a threshold which allows death to be recognized as a transition into another political, social, and poetic world" (166). Parenthetically, this transition, with its sociopolitical emphasis, is quite different from the transition (into the still-withheld beginning of Western thought) for which Heidegger saw the figure of the poet, and in particular Hölderlin, as a precursor.

3. F. Hölderlin, "Anmerkungen zum Oedipus" and "Anmerkungen zur Antigonä," SW II, 849–57, and 913–21, respectively. For English translations of these texts, see *Friedrich Hölderlin: Essays and Letters on Theory*, trans. and ed. Thomas Pfau (Albany: State University of New York Press, 1988), 101–16. Given the density and difficulty of the texts, any translation is an interpretation. In keeping with English usage, I have italicized *Oedipus* and *Antigone* in citing Hölderlin's titles in translation, but his German has been left as is.

4. *F. Hölderlin to Casimir Ulrich Böhlendorff*, 4 December 1801, letter 237, and undated, letter 241, SW II, 459–62 and 466–68. Dennis J. Schmidt offers a full translation of the first letter in Appendix C to his *On Germans and Other Greeks*.

5. *Sophoclis Tragoediae Septem* (Frankfurt: Braubach, 1555). Of the two simultaneous editions that may be thus referenced, Hölderlin seems to have used the *quarto* edition with added *scholia*. The additional textual sources that he seems also to have made use of, particularly for *Oedipus Tyrannos*, have not been identified.

6. SW II offers a detailed textual commentary which, as the editors note, documents for the first time the scope of textual corruptions in the *Brubachiana* edition of *Antigone* relative to Hölderlin's translation. Norbert von Hellingrath already commented on the "strange mixture of intimacy with the Greek language, and a lively grasp of its beauty and character, with ignorance of its most simple rules and a complete lack of grammatical exactitude" that was characteristic of Hölderlin (whose schooling, geared to the career of a minister, emphasized Latin, and probably also Hebrew, over the classical Greek that he loved). See SW II, 1327.

7. SW II, 1327.

8. Bernhard Böschenstein, "Hölderlins 'Oedipus'—Hölderlins 'Antigonä'," in *Hölderlin und die Moderne*, ed. Gerhard Kurz, Valérie Lawitschka, and Jürgen Wertheimer (Tübingen: Attempto Verlag, 1995), 224–39 [225]. Böschenstein also offers here a summary discussion of the philological researches of Friedrich Beissner and the older, still important interpretations by Karl Reinhardt, Wolfgang Binder, and Wolfgang Schadewaldt.

9. As Gerhard Kurz points out, however, eighteenth-century aesthetics and poetics, for all its infatuation with incalculable subjectivity, "never abandoned the goal to find laws for art." See Gerhard Kurz, "Poetische Logik: Zu Hölderlins Anmerkungen zu 'Oedipus' und 'Antigone,'" in *Jenseits des Idealismus: Hölderlins letzte Homburger Jahre (1804–1806)*, ed. Christoph Jamme and Otto Pöggeler (Bonn: Bouvier, 1988), 83–99 (84).

10. *Hölderlin to Wilmans*, 2 April 1804, SW II, 472f.

11. SW II, 850.

12. Line references to the Greek text are to R. D. Dawe, ed., *Sophocles: Oedipus Rex* (Cambridge: Cambridge University Press, 1982), which will be cited as OT. I have also consulted the English translation by Robert Fagles in *Sophocles: Three Theban Plays* (Harmondsworth: Penguin, 1982).

13. SW II, 851.

14. SW II, 852.

15. SW III, 466.

16. See SW II, 853f.

17. SW II, 852.

18. SW II, 856.

19. Reiner Schürmann, "Ultimate Double Binds," in James Risser, ed., *Heidegger Toward the Turn*, 248.

20. See note 9, above.

21. Hölderlin translates more pointedly: "Was fürchtet denn der Mensch, der mit dem Glück / Es hält? Von nichts gibts eine Ahnung deutlich . . ." ("What then does a man fear who puts his trust in fortune? Of nothing is there any distinct presentiment . . ."). Here man is not just ruled by chance, but—if he has any sense—he stays in league with luck or good fortune, and thus with happiness.

22. David Farrell Krell, "Hölderlin's Tragic Heroines: Jocasta, Antigone, Niobe, Danaë." This paper was presented as the André Schuwer lecture at the 2002 meeting of the Society for Existential Philosophy and Phenomenology; and I thank the author for making it available to me in its still unpublished state.

23. Gerhard Kurz, "Poetische Logik," 89.

24. "'*Oedipus auf Colonus*' . . . ," 163f.

25. *Op. cit.*, 166.

26. SW II, 256.

27. "La césure du spéculatif," 66.

28. Concerning this last quotation, see note to chapter epigraph, above. See Krell, *Lunar Voices*, 21, note 21. Krell's reference is to Dastur, *Hölderlin: tragédie et modernité*.

29. SW II, 856f.

CHAPTER SIX. DYS-LIMITATION AND THE "PATRIOTIC TURNING": SOPHOCLES' *ANTIGONE*

Epigraph from William Butler Yeats, *Words for Music Perhaps: XI, "From the 'Antigone'."*

1. SW II, 913.

2. See Aristotle, *Poetics*, 51b.1

3. This censure of philosophy contrasts with his earlier enthusiasm for it. See, for instance, the correspondence cited by Manfred Frank in his "Hölderlins philosophische Grundlagen," *Hölderlin und die Moderne*, 174–94 (175).

4. SW II, 915.

5. SW II, 914. The "unwritten wilderness" here echoes both Antigone's respect for the unwritten divine laws and the late Hölderlin's own concern for "the firm letter."

6. Line references to the Greek text of *Antigone* are to Sir Richard C. Jebb, ed., *The Antigone of Sophocles*, with a commentary abridged by E. S. Shuckburgh, 8th ed. (Cambridge: Cambridge University Press, 1990). I have also consulted Robert Fagles's English translation in *Sophocles: Three Theban Plays*.

7. On unwritten laws, compare Pericles' Funeral Oration in Thucydides, *The History of the Peloponnesian War*, ii: 37. This text was important to Hölderlin, who meditated and commented on it.

8. Lacoue-Labarthe writes that he hesitated somewhat to turn to *Antigone*, not just because "I thought about Schelling's consternation before the translation of Sophocles which, he wrote to Hegel, 'betrays his [Hölderlin's] mental unhinging.' In fact, rather because I thought about Hegel himself, about Hegel's icy silence—[Hegel] who went on to write, in the very year following the publication of the Remarks, these pages of *The Phenomenology of Spirit* consecrated to *Antigone*, which have shaped . . . the modern interpretation of tragedy." "La césure . . . ," 56.

9. While philosophical attention has been paid to Hölderlin's "Remarks," his *translation* of *Antigone*, which is far more idiosyncratic than that of *Oedipus Tyrannos*, has been philosophically ignored. Yet there is the possibility that, notwithstanding Schelling's negative judgment, *Hölderlin's very translation* could have exerted a certain influence upon Hegel's thought, at least by suggestion (Hegel, however, does not quote from it in his discussion of *Antigone* in the *Phenomenology of Spirit*).

10. I refer primarily to G. W. F. Hegel's *Vorlesungen über die Aesthetik*, III, and *Phänomenologie des Geistes*, 324–54. For an excellent discussion, see Kathleen Wright, "Heidegger on Hegel's Antigone: The Memory of Gender and the Forgetfulness of Ethical Difference," in *Endings: Questions of Memory in Hegel and Heidegger*, ed. Rebecca Comay and John McCumber (Evanston: Northwestern University Press, 1999), 160–73 (with Notes, 237–39).

11. F. Dastur, *Hölderlin: tragédie et modernité*, 106f.

12. *Op. cit.*, 195.

13. Hölderlin's translation here uncharacteristically mutes rather than intensifies Sophocles' diction: He has Antigone say: "Wer weiss, da kann doch drunt' ein andrer Brauch sein" ("Who knows, a different custom might obtain below"); SW II, 914. "Naïve" is not, for him, a derogatory term; it indicates one of the fundamental poetic tones. Concerning the place of different variants of the naïve tone in epic and tragic poetry, see his schematic fragment "Wechsel der Töne" ("Change of Tones), SW II, 524–26.

14. *Op. cit.*, 106.

15. SW, 914. I depart here from the reading of the editors of SW, to the effect that it is man who is the object that spirit is interested in, so that man becomes objectified (SW II,1475). Lawrence Ryan's reading, in "Hölderlins Antigone: 'Wie es vom griechischen zum hesperischen geht," in *Jenseits des Idealismus*, 103–21, similarly opposes man as "object" to spirit (105). The reference of the masculine nominative singular personal pronoun *er* ("he/it") in Hölderlin's text is ambiguous; but, whether it is referred to man or to spirit matters little, since man is spoken of *insofar as he is seized by spirit*. Such "seizure," however, does not warrant construing man as the object spirit is interested in; the object is better understood as the human being's concrete object of concern once he or she is seized by spirit.

16. SW II, 915.

17. See E. R. Dodds, *The Greeks and the Irrational* (Berkeley: University of California Press, 1951).

18. *Hölderlin to Böhlendorff*, 4 December 1801, SW III, 460.

19. SW II, 807.

20. Letter 237, to Böhlendorff, SW III, 467.

21. SW III, 469.

22. SW II, 460. Hölderlin's references to the "national" are not politically fraught (as tends to be indicated by his use of the noun form *das Nationelle*, rather than *das Nationale*).

23. Dastur, *Hölderlin* . . . , 27. As to the ruin of Greek civilization, Dastur refers to Hölderlin's late hymn *Griechenland*.

24. SW III, 466.

25. SW II, 915.

26. SW II, 917.

27. SW II, 920.

28. SW II, 917.

29. SW II, 919.

30. See here Jean-François Marquet, "Structure de la mythologie hölderlinienne," in *L'Herne: Hölderlin*, ed. Jean-François Courtine (Paris: Editions de l'Herne, 1989), 352–67.

31. See Claudia Albert, "'Dient Kulturarbeit dem Sieg?'—Hölderlin-Rezeption von 1933–1945," in *Hölderlin und die Moderne*, 352–69. Among the factual details one learns from this study (which is, however, concerned with explaining, and not merely documenting, Hölderlin's posthumous Nazification) is that, on the one hundreth anniversary of the poet's death in 1943, *The Death of Empedocles* was performed in Würtemberg. The Sophocles translations, however, seem not to have attracted much attention in this historical context.

32. SW II, 918.

33. Beda Allemann, "Hölderlin entre les Anciens et les Modernes," trans. François Fédier, in *L'Herne: Hölderlin*, 297–321 (304).

34. This discussion stretches from SW II, 919 to 920 and also explains why, in the tragic turning, mere neutrality is excluded.

35. See A, 211–14; 278f; and the note of warning in the first *stasimon*, A, 368–71.

36. SW II, 857.

37. Nicole Loraux's erudite and insightful study, "La main d'Antigone," *Métis*, I:2 (1986): 165–96, focuses on the compounds of *auto-* that are dominant in the Sophoclean text, particularly on ἀυτόχειρ ("by one's own hand"). Hölderlin's translation of the five Sophoclean lines containing this compound, as well as of the closely related line 14 (SW II, 863), is remarkably sensitive to the nuances of Sophoclean diction, except for one instance (A, 306; SW II, 871). I thank Professor Michael Naas for making this text available to me.

38. SW II, 891.

39. SW II, 915.

40. SW II, 916.

41. The discussion here is based on SW II, 916f.

42. For the legend of Boreas and Oreihyia, see Plato, *Phdr.*, 229b–e. Sophocles does not name Cleopatra but relies on the audience's recognition of the cruel tale of her sons' eyes being stabbed out by her husband's new wife.

43. SW II, 896 and 916.

44. SW II, 916.

45. Compare SW II, 816 and 916.

46. SW II, 917.

47. *Op. cit.*, 191, 198. Loraux's complex and brilliant analysis also explores the symbolism of Antigone's repetition of Jokasta's death (noting Sophocles's emphasis on the maternal figure in that he likens Antigone to a bereaved mother bird, and by having her compare herself to Niobe), pointing out that she dies of "the desire of the mother." She further comments on Antigone's "lapidation," in that the rock-hewn tomb is said to envelop her, in the manner of the veil that becomes the instrument of her death and also, as a concealing garment, its symbol. Hölderlin's introduction of the figure of the desert distracts the reader from this lapidation (suffered literally by Niobe).

48. See SW II, 918–19.

49. SW II, 918.

50. Lacoue-Labarthe, *L'imitation des modernes*, 83–84.

51. SW II, 919.

52. SW II, 921.

53. *Ibid.*

54. F. Dastur, *Le retournement natal*, 137. Dasstur notes here (in a chapter on "Nature and the Sacred") that Hölderlin's poetry is set apart by its hymnic tonality from the lyric poetry of the age, for which feeling had become the key word.

CHAPTER SEVEN. FROM AN AGONISTIC OF POWERS TO A HOMECOMING: HEIDEGGER, HÖLDERLIN, AND SOPHOCLES

Epigraph from F. Hölderlin, *Am Quell der Donau* (*At the Source of the Danube*), GW, I, 322.

1. Martin Heidegger, *Einführung in die Metaphysik*, 4th ed. (Tübingen: Niemeyer, 1976), 81. This work will be referred to as EM.

2. *Ibid.*

3. Parmenides, **ΠΕΡΙ ΦΥΣΕΩΣ**, Fragment 3

4. EM, 116.

5. Otto Pöggeler also points this out in his "Die engen Schranken unserer noch kinderähnlichen Kultur." See p. 40. This is presumbly part of the violence that Heidegger acknowledges doing to the text. Pöggeler also notes that, for Hölderlin, the wider context of interpretation (the idea that those who are great fall most precipitously) here reflects the corruption of his textual source (on which see ch. 5, below), which transforms *to mē kalon* ("what is not beautiful/noble") into *to men kalon* ("the beautiful/noble"). See p. 41. Heidegger, though far from being limited to a corrupt textual source, nonetheless follows Hölderlin's interpretation on this point.

6. EM, 117. My translation of Heidegger's German here is also somewhat artful, so as to convey the deliberate echoing of *fahren* ("travelling, voyaging") in *Erfahrung* ("experience").

7. *Ibid.*

8. EM, 122.

9. EM, 123.

10. Heidegger's prominent use of *reissen* and *Riss* here recalls the prominence of these same terms in his contemporaneous essay "The Origin of the Work of Art," GA, 5.

11. EM, 123.

12. EM, 124.

13. EM, 125.

14. EM, 96f.

15. Martin Heidegger, *Nietzsche*, 4th ed., 2 vols. (Pfullingen: Neske, 1961, 1963); vol. I, 205.

16. *Ibid.*

17. Jean-François Courtine, "Of Tragic Metaphor," trans. Jonathan Derbyshire, *Philosophy and Tragedy*, 59–77 (60). See also Friedrich Schelling, *Briefe über Dogma-*

tismus und Kritizismus, in *Friedrich Wilhelm Josef Schelling, Werke*, ed. H. Bucher, W. J. Jacobs, and A. Pieper (Stuttgart: Frommann-Holzboog, 1982), vol. III; and Peter Szondi, "The Notion of the Tragic in Schelling, Hölderlin, and Hegel," in *On Textual Understanding and Other Essays*, trans. Harvey Mendelsohn (Minneapolis: University of Minnesota Press, 1986), 43–55.

18. Courtine, *op. cit.*, 60. See Friedrich Schelling, *Philosophie der Kunst, Werke*, V.

19. M. Heidegger, "Zu Hölderlins Empedokles Bruchstücken," in *Zu Hölderlins Griechenlandsreisen*, GA, 75 (2000), 331–40; and M. Heidegger, "Der Spruch des Anaximander," *Holzwege*, 4th ed. (Frankfurt a.M.: Klostermann, 1950). See the discussion of the Anaximander text in chapter one above. The reference is to GA, 53, 1.

20. GA, 53, 79.

21. GA, 53, 70.

22. GA, 53, 87.

23. GA, 53, 89.

24. GA, 53, 95f. I put "metaphysics" in quotation marks because the term is used today, in Heidegger's negative sense, with excessive facility. Moreover, I question whether Heidegger's understanding of "metaphysics," in this sense, does justice to certain aspects of the Western metaphysical tradition.

25. GA, 53, 98.

26. M. Heidegger, *Parmenides* (*Freiburger Vorlesung, Wintersemester 1942/43*), GA, 54 (1982, 1990). See pp. 130–44.

27. The Greek verb has a more dynamic sense than does "to be." This is reflected in Heidegger's translation of the Sophoclean verse in question. Concerning the notion of the pole or poles as a Heideggerian echo (problematized, as always) in the poetry and prose of Paul Celan, see my *Heidegger and the Poets: Poiēsis, Sophia, Technē* (Atlantic Highlands: Humanities Press, 1992), ch. 7.

28. GA, 53, 100.

29. GA, 54, 133.

30. GA, 54, 134. See also chapter 1, above, on the importance of Burckhardt's view of the *polis* to Nietzsche.

31. GA, 53, 107.

32. GA, 53, 118.

33. GA, 53, 122.

34. GA, 53, 128.

35. GA, 53, 128.

36. GA, 53, 129.

37. GA, 53, 140.

38. Compare GA, 53, 150.

39. GA, 53, 144.

40. GA, 53, 154f. See also 169f.

41. GA, 53, 155.

42. Even though Heidegger occasionally cites Sappho, her pure lyricism (and sustained focus on the singular) would not count, for him, as the sort of poetic instauration he attributes to poets such as Homer, Pindar, or Hölderlin himself.

43. "Remarks on Antigone," SW II, 919f.

44. For Hölderlin, it is above all (as noted in chapter 6, above) Haimon who cannot reconcile his end with his beginning.

EPILOGUE

1. Reiner Schürmann, *Des hégémonies brisées*, 778.

2. "Remarks on Oedipus," SW II, 851.

3. "Remarks on Antigone," SW II, 914.

4. Baruch (Benedictus de) Spinoza, *Tractatus Theologico-Politicus*, ed. and trans. Samuel Shirley (Leiden: Brill, 1989).

5. "Remarks on Antigone," SW II, 916f. Concerning "The General Ground," see ch. 3, above.

6. F. Hölderlin, *Der Archipelagus*, SW II, 253–63. The hymn (written in trochaic hexameters, an exalted diction which translation cannot reproduce), seems to have been written in 1800–1801. Heidegger also cites these verses in GA, 53, 88.

Bibliography

Note: This bibliography does not seek to be comprehensive, nor to provide a guide to the literature. It restricts itself to listing works that have been directly pertinent to the writing of this book. Contributions to the edited books included in the bibliography have not been separately referenced. Such references, can, however, be found in the Notes.

HÖLDERLIN: TEXTS

Hölderlin, Johann Christian Friedrich. *Sämtliche Werke*. "Grosse Stuttgarter Ausgabe." Edited by Friedrich Beissner, followed by Adolph Beck. 15 vols. Stuttgart: Kohlhammer, 1946–1957.

———. *Sämtliche Werke*. "Frankfurter historisch-kritische Ausgabe." Edited by D. E. Sattler and W. Greddeck. 20 vols. Frankfurt: Roter Stern, 1975.

———. *Sämtliche Werke und Briefe*. Edited by Jochen Schmidt, in collaboration with Katharina Grätz (vol. 2) and Wolfgang Behschnitt (vol. 3). 3 vols. Frankfurt a.M.: Deutsche Klassiker Verlag, 1992–1994.

Pfau, Thomas, ed. and trans. *Hölderlin: Essays and Letters on Theory*. Albany: State University of New York Press, 1988.

GREEK TRAGEDY, MYTHOLOGY, AND PHILOSOPHY

Aristotle. *Poetics, with the Tractatus Coislinianus, Reconstruction of Poetics II, and the Fragment of the On Poets*. Translated by Chris Turner. Indianapolis, IN: Hackett, 1987.

———. *Poetics*. Cambridge, MA: Loeb Classical Library, 1932.

Blondell, Ruby, trans. *Sophocles's Antigone*. Newburyport, MA: Focus Publishing, 1988.

Bollack, Jean. *Empédocle*. 3 vols. Paris: Minuit, 1965–1969.

Burnet, Ioannes, ed. *Platonis Opera*. "Oxford Classical Texts." Oxford: Oxford University Press, 1901.

Burkert, Walter. *Homo necans: Interpretationen altgriechischer Opferriten und Mythen*. Berlin: de Gruyter, 1972.

———. *Structure and History of Greek Mythology and Ritual*. Berkeley: University of California Press, 1979.

Buxton, R. G. A. *Persuasion in Greek Tragedy. A Study of Peitho*. Berkeley: University of California Press, 1982.

Calasso, Roberto. *The Marriage of Cadmus and Harmony*. New York: Vintage, 1993.

Cooper, John M., ed. *Plato: Complete Works*. Indianapolis, IN: Hackett, 1997.

Dawe, R. D., ed. *Sophocles: Oedipus Rex*. Cambridge: Cambridge University Press, 1982.

Diogenes Laërtius. *Lives of the Philosophers*. Translated by A. Robert Caponigri. Chicago: Gateway, 1969.

Dodds, E. R. *The Greeks and the Irrational*. Berkeley: University of California Press, 1951.

Freeman, Kathleen. *Ancilla to the Pre-Socratic Philosophers*. Cambridge: Harvard University Press, 1971.

Furley, David. J., and R. E. Allen, eds. *The Pre-Socratics: A Collection of Critical Essays*. 2 vols. London: Routledge, 1970.

Grene, David, and Richmond Lattimore, eds. *The Complete Greek Tragedies*. Chicago: University of Chicago Press, 1969.

Jebb, Sir Richard C. *The Antigone of Sophocles*. Abridged by E. S. Shuckburgh. 18th edition. Cambridge: Cambridge University Press, 1990.

Kennedy, George. *The Art of Persuasion in Greece*. Princeton, NJ: Princeton University Press, 1963.

Long, A. A., ed. *The Cambridge Companion to Early Greek Philosophy*. Cambridge: Cambridge University Press, 1999.

Loraux, Nicole. "La main d'Antigone." *Métis* I: 2 (1986): 165–96.

———. *Tragic Ways of Killing a Woman*. Translated by Anthony Forster. Cambridge: Harvard University Press, 1987.

Mourelatos, Alexander P. D., ed. *The Pre-Socratics: A Collection of Critical Essays*. 2nd revised edition. Princeton, NJ: Princeton University Press, 1993.

Naas, Michael. *Turning from Persuasion to Philosophy: a Reading of Homer's Iliad*. Atlantic Highlands, NJ: Humanities Press, 1995.

Nussbaum, Martha C. *The Fragility of Goodness: Luck and Ethics in Greek Tragedy and Philosophy*. Cambridge: Cambridge University Press, 1986.

Vernant, Jean-Pierre. *Mythe et pensée chez les grecs: études de psychologie historique*. 2 vols. Paris: Éditions la Découverte, 1972.

Vernant, Jean-Pierre, and Pierre Vidal-Naquet. *Tragedy and Myth in Ancient Greece*. Translated by Janet Lloyd. Atlantic Highlands, NJ: Humanities Press, 1981.

Wright, M. R. *Empedocles: The Extant Fragments*. New Haven: Yale University Press, 1981.

OTHER LITERATURE

Allemann, Beda. *Hölderlin und Heidegger*. Zürich: Atlantis Verlag, 1954.

Arnold, Matthew. *Empedocles on Aetna*. In J. H. Buckley and J. B. Woods, eds., *Poetry of the Victorian Period*, 443–56. Glenview, IL: Scott, Foresman and Company, 1955.

Babich, Babette E. *Words in Blood Like Flowers: Poetry, Philosophy, Music, and Eros in Hölderlin, Nietzsche, and Heidegger*. Albany: State University of New York Press, forthcoming, 1996.

Beaufret, Jean. *Hölderlin et Sophocle*. Paris: Gérard Montfort, 1983.

Beistegui, Miguel de, and Simon Sparks, eds. *Philosophy and Tragedy*. London: Routledge, 2000.

Benjamin, Walter. *Der Ursprung des deutschen Trauerspiels*. Frankfurt a.M.: Suhrkamp, 1978.

———. *Gesammelte Schriften*. Edited by A. Tiedemann and Hermann Schweppenhäuser. Frankfurt a.M.: Suhrkamp, 1980.

Böschenstein, Bernhard et al., eds. *Hölderlin—Jahrbuch*. Vol. 31. Eggingen: Edition Isele, 1998–1999.

Bourdieu, Pierre. *The Political Ontology of Martin Heidegger*. Translated by Peter Collier. Stanford: Stanford University Press, 1991.

Chanter, Tina. "Antigone's Dilemma." In R. Bernasconi and S. Critchley, eds. *Re-Reading Levinas*, 130–46. Bloomington, IN: Indiana University Press, 1991.

Comay, Rebecca, and John McCumber, eds. *Endings: Questions of Memory in Hegel and Heidegger*. Evanston, IL: Northwestern University Press, 1999.

Courtine, Jean-François, ed. *L'Herne: Hölderlin*. Paris: Editions de l'Herne, 1989.

Dastur, Françoise. *Hölderlin: Le retournement natal*. Fougères, La Versanne: encre marine, 1997.

———. *Dire le temps*. La Versanne: encre marine, 1994.

Derrida, Jacques. "Plato's Pharmacy." In *Disseminations*. Translated by Barbara Johnson, 61–172. Chicago: University of Chicago Press, 1981.

Fóti, Véronique M. *Heidegger and the Poets: Poiēsis, Sophia, Technē*. Atlantic Highlands, NJ: Humanities Press, 1992.

———. "Hölderlin, Johann Christian Friedrich." In *The Edinburgh Encyclopedia of Modern Theory and Criticism*. Edited by Julian Wolfreys, 29–36. Edinburgh: Edinburgh University Press, 2002.

———. *Vision's Invisibles: Philosophical Explorations*. Albany: State University of New York Press, 2003.

Gellrich, Michelle. *Tragedy and Theory: the Problem of Conflict Since Aristotle*. Princeton: Princeton University Press, 1988.

Haar, Michel. *The Song of the Earth: Heidegger and the Ground of the History of Being*. Translated by Reginald Lilly. Bloomington, IN: Indiana University Press, 1987.

Haverkamp, Anselm. *Laub voll Trauer: Hölderlins späte Allegorie*. Munich: Fink, 1991.

Hegel, G. W. F. *Werke in zwanzig Bänden*. "Theorie Werkausgabe." 20 vols. Frankfurt a.M.: Suhrkamp, 1970.

Heidegger, Martin. *Geamtausgabe* (GA). Frankfurt a.M.: Klostermann, 1976–.

GA 4: *Erläuterungen zu Hölderlins Dichtung* (1982).

GA 5: *Holzwege* (1977).

GA 9: *Wegmarken* (1976).

GA 29/30: *Die Grundbegriffe der Metaphysik. Welt—Endlichkeit—Einsamkeit* (1983).

GA 39: *Hölderlins Hymnen "Germanien" und "Der Rhein"* (1980).

GA 40: *Einführung in die Metaphysik* (1983).

GA 43: *Nietzsche: Der Wille zur Macht als Kunst* (1985).

GA 52: *Hölderlins Hymne "Andenken"* (1982).

GA 53: *Hölderlins Hymne "Der Ister"* (1984).

GA 54: *Parmenides* (1982).

GA 65: *Beiträge zur Philosophie* (Vom Ereignis) (2003).

GA 75: *Zu Hölderlin. Griechenlandreisen* (2002).

Hölscher, Uvo. *Empedokles und Hölderlin*. Frankfurt a.M.: Insel Verlag, 1965.

Irigaray, Luce. *Speculum of the Other Woman*. Translated by G. C. Gill. Ithaca, NY: Cornell University Press, 1985.

Jacob, David C., ed. *The Presocratics After Heidegger*. Albany: State University of New York Press, 1999.

Jamme, Christoph, and Otto Pöggeler, eds. *Jenseits des Idealismus: Hölderlins letzte Homburger Jahre* (1804–1806). Bonn: Bouvier, 1988.

Krell, David Farrell. *Daimon Life: Heidegger and Life-Philosophy*. Bloomington, IN: Indiana University Press, 1992.

———. "Hölderlin's Tragic Heroines: Jocasta, Antigone, Niobe, Danaë." Presented as the André Schuwer Lecture at the 2002 conference of the Society for Phenomenology and Existential Philosophy.

———. *Lunar Voices: Of Tragedy, Poetry, Fiction, and Thought*. Chicago: University of Chicago Press, 1995.

Kurz, Gerhard, Valérie Lawitschka, and Jürgen Wertheimer, eds. *Hölderlin und die Moderne*. Tübingen: Attempto Verlag, 1995.

Lacoue-Labarthe, Philippe. *L'Imitation des Modernes: Typographies II*. Paris: Galilée, 1986.

———. *Heidegger, Art and Politcs*. Translated by Chris Turner. London: Blackwell, 1990.

Nietzsche, Friedrich. *Sämtliche Werke*. "Kritische Studienausgabe." Edited by Giorgio Colli and Mazzino Montinari. 15 vols. Berlin: de Gruyter, 1988.

Preminger, A., and D. V. F. Brogan, eds. *The New Princeton Encyclopedia of Poetry and Poetics*. New York: MJF Books, 1993.

Pöggeler, Otto. *Heidegger*. Cologne: Kiepenhauer & Witsch, 1969.

———. *The Paths of Heidegger's Life and Thought*. Translated by John Bailiff. Atlantic Highlands, NJ: Humanities Press, 1987.

Risser, James, ed. *Heidegger Toward the Turn: Essays on the Work of the 1930's*. Albany: State University of New York Press, 1999.

Sallis, John. *Crossings: Nietzsche and the Space of Tragedy*. Chicago: University of Chicago Press, 1991.

———, ed. "Heidegger and Hölderlin." *Research in Phenomenology* 19 (1989).

Schelling, Friedrich Wilhelm Josef von. *Werke*. Edited by H. Buchner, W. G. Jacobs, and A. Pieper. 8 vols. Stuttgart: Frommann Holzboog, 1982.

Schmidt, Dennis J. *On Germans and Other Greeks: Tragedy and Ethical Life*. Bloomington, IN: Indiana University Press, 2001.

Schürmann, Reiner. *Des hégémonies brisées*. Mauvezin: Trans-Europ-Repress, 1996.

———. *Heidegger on Being and Acting: from Principles to Anarchy*. Translated by Marie-Christine Gros. Bloomington, IN: Indiana University Press, 1987.

Steiner, George. *Antigones*. Oxford: Clarendon, 1986.

———. *Language and Silence: Essays on Language, Literature, and the Inhuman*. London: Atheneum, 1970.

Szondi, Peter. *On Textual Understanding, and Other Essays*. Translated by Harvey Mendelsohn. Minneapolis, MN: University of Minnesota Press, 1986.

———. *Schriften*. Edited by Jean Bollack. Frankfurt a.M. Suhrkamp, 1979.

Taminiaux, Jacques. *Le théatre des philosophes: la tragédie, l'être, l'action*. Grenoble: Millon, 1995.

Wegenast, Margarethe. *Hölderlins Spinoza-Rezeption, und ihre Bedeutung für die Konzeption des "Hyperion."* Tübingen: Niemeyer, 1990.

Index of Persons

This index contains not only the names of historical and living individuals, but also those of tragic characters and Greek deities.

Index of Topics